To My Students

This Study Guide is designed to help you study *Abnormal Psychology, 9th Edition* by Davison & Neale. Each chapter in this guide provides a variety of aids to make your studying easier and more effective.

Overview sections place the chapter in context by describing its relationship to the chapters that precede and follow it.

Chapter Summary sections, not surprisingly, summarize the chapter.

Study Objectives list the important ideas or concepts to be learned in the chapter.

Key Terms provide a place for you to write in definitions of technical words introduced in the chapter. Typically, these terms are boldfaced in the text.

Study Questions are questions for you to answer as you read each section of the text. The Study Guide provides space for you to write your answers to each question. Research indicates that actually writing the answers is an effective way to study.

Self-Test provides a way for you to check your knowledge of the chapter. The Self-Test questions cover the content specified by the Study Questions, except for an occasional asterisked (*) test question.

The Study Guide begins with a chapter on *Studying in This Course (and in Other Courses Too)*. This chapter is based on my experiences helping my students improve their study skills. It describes a study method (SQ4R) you can use to improve your study skills. It also provides suggestions for coping with common study problems. I hope you'll find this chapter helpful.

Abnormal psychology is a fascinating, but complex, topic for many students. Hopefully, this Study Guide will make your studying easier and more effective. It is based on the experiences, comments, and criticisms of hundreds of students who have used it in my classes. I invite you to join them in offering suggestions for further improvements.

Douglas Hindman
Berea, Kentucky

CONTENTS

Introduction:
Studying in This Course
(and in Other Courses Too)

Overview

I'm convinced, though it might be hard to prove, that few students get bad grades because they're dumb. There is little in the average college curriculum (including abnormal psychology) that's beyond the intellectual capacities of most college students. I'm convinced most students get poor grades because they don't know how to study.

Being a student is a job. The hours are long and the pay is terrible but it's still a job. The payoff is the knowledge you gain and the grades you get. You've been at this "job" for many years, and you're probably not through with it. If this is to be your job you might consider how to become really good at it. Are you learning? Are you working efficiently and getting the results you should?

This Study Guide incorporates features to help you develop good study skills. If you spend a little time consciously working on your study skills, you can help the process along.

This chapter is intended to help you review and improve your study skills. The first part of the chapter describes a system, SQ4R, which you can use in this, or almost any, course. The second part of the chapter contains suggestions for dealing with common study problems.

The SQ4R Study System

The following is one variation of a study method called "SQ4R" (Survey, Question, Read, Write, Recite, Review). If you're not used to it, it may seem a bit complicated at first. If you check around, though, you will find that the "good" students are already using it or a similar system. Research shows that SQ4R works. It takes a bit of extra effort to get used to, but remember that studying is a skill and that learning any skill (like typing, driving, and playing ball) takes time and practice. You will find, though, that your efforts will pay off in both this and your other courses.

As you begin to study a new chapter, use the following steps:

Survey

First, survey the entire chapter briefly. Spend a few minutes getting a general idea of the material. Look over the titles, pictures, introduction, and summary in the text. Read the overview, chapter summary, and essential concepts in this Study Guide. While doing so, ask yourself what you will be studying. Figure out how the text is organized to cover the topic. Don't read the chapter in detail yet. This brief survey will help you focus your attention and become familiar with new vocabulary and concepts. Research suggests that initially surveying the chapter can reduce your overall study time by 40%.

Question

Take the first portion of the chapter and ask yourself what you are about to study. The study questions in this Study Guide will help you formulate this question. In other courses, take the main heading or topic and turn it into a question.

Read

Then, read the first portion of the text looking for the answer to your question. It is important that you actively seek the answer as you read. Deliberately try *not* to read every word. Instead, read for answers.

Typically a text will make several points regarding each general topic. Look for words indicating these points such as, "first," "furthermore," or "finally". Generally a paragraph contains one idea. Additional paragraphs may elaborate on or illustrate the point. You may find it helpful to number each point in the text as you find it.

Write

Write down the answer in the space below the study question in your guide. In other courses, take study notes. This step is critical. By writing the answer you confirm that you actually understand it. Occasionally, when you try to write down your answer, you'll discover you don't understand the idea well enough to put it into words. That's okay. Go back and read some more until you figure it out.

As you write the answer, strive to use as few words as possible. Being concise is important. Try to come up with a few key words that convey the idea. When you can condense a long portion of text into a few key words that express the whole idea, you know you understand the concept clearly. The few key words you write down will be meaningful to you so you will remember them. Do not write complete sentences or elaborate excessively. The fewer words you can use, the better you probably understand and will remember the concept.

When you finish, go on to the next study question. Read, write, and repeat until you finish.

Recite

After you finish the chapter, go back and quiz yourself. Do this aloud. Actively speaking and listening to yourself will help you remember. Look at each question and try to repeat the answer without looking. Cover your answers with a sheet of paper so you don't peek accidentally. If you've done the earlier steps well, this won't take much time.

Review

Set aside a few minutes every week to recite the material again. Put several questions together and try to recite all the answers to a whole general topic. Do this regularly and you'll find it takes little time to refresh yourself for an exam.

Get with a classmate to quiz each other, or ask a friend to read the questions and tell you if your answers make sense. This step helps you understand (not just memorize) the ideas. As you discuss answers with someone else, you develop new ways of looking at the material. This can be especially helpful when the test questions aren't phrased quite the way you expected.

Coping with Study Problems

The previous section of this chapter described an active study technique that has proven useful to many students. This section talks about common study complaints and what to do about them.

Finding the Time

Does it seem like you never have time to study — or that you study all the time and still aren't getting results? Admittedly, study takes time, but let's look at the matter.

The traditional rule of thumb is that you should study two hours outside class for every hour in class. If that sounds like a lot, consider this. The average college student class load is 15 semester hours. If you study two hours for each class hour that's 30 additional hours for a "work week" of 45 hours.

If you have trouble finding that 45 hours, it's time to look at how you spend your time. Make a "time log". You can copy the time log at the end of this chapter or make one of your own. Use it to record how you spend your time for a week or so. Don't try to change what you're doing. Just record it.

After a week or so, review your log to see how you're using your time. There are 90 hours between 8 A.M. and 11 P.M. in a six-day week. If you devote half those hours to the "job" of being a student, you'll have 45 hours left. It's your time.

You may want to schedule your time differently. You'll need to decide what works for your style and situation. If you set up a schedule, be sure to include time for things you really enjoy as well as time to eat, do your laundry, etc.

Schedule adequate study time and actually spend it studying. If you get everything done and have time left over, use it to get ahead in one of your classes. When your study time is over, you should be able to enjoy other activities without worrying about your "job".

Getting Started

Do you find it difficult to actually get down to work when it's study time? Many students find it helpful to find or make a specific "study place". It could be a desk in your room, the library, or any place where you won't be disturbed and have access to your books and materials.

Use your study place *only* to study. If it *has* to be a place where you do other things, change it in some way when you use it to study. For example, if you use the kitchen table, clear it off and place a study light on it before you start to study. If you're interrupted, leave your study place until the interruption is over and you can return to studying.

If you do this, you'll soon get into the habit of doing nothing but studying in your study place and will be able to get to work as soon as you sit down.

Reading the Material

Some students believe that effective study means to "read the chapter" three or four times. This could be called the "osmosis approach" to studying. You expose yourself to the words in the text and hope something will soak in — like getting a sun tan. This approach does *not* work.

If you just "read the chapter" you'll often realize you've been looking at words but have no idea what they mean. If you come to a difficult idea, you're likely to skip over it. When you reread the chapter, you're likely to recall that the idea was difficult and skip over it again. The result is that you end up having read the chapter three or four times without understanding most of it.

Instead, use an active study technique like the SQ4R system described earlier. Research indicates that active study techniques can dramatically increase how quickly you learn material and how much of it you recall.

Underlining the Text

Many students underline (or highlight) their texts. Underlining works well — sometimes. For most people, underlining is not as efficient as taking notes. The danger in underlining is that you tend to underline things to be learned later rather than learning them now. Thus, you can end up with half the chapter underlined and none of it learned. If you *must* underline, try to underline as few words as possible in the same way as the "key words" approach described in the "Write" section earlier. Avoid used textbooks that someone else underlined. They may have been a poor underliner. More importantly, the value of underlining (like the value of taking notes) is in doing it yourself and in learning what's important in the process.

Reading Speed

Slow reading can lead to a number of problems. Most obviously, it takes too long to get through the material. More importantly, you lose interest before you get to the main point. You forget the first part of an idea before you get to the end. (You "lose the forest for the trees".) You may not understand a concept unless it's clearly stated in one sentence. You may misinterpret material because you take so long getting through it that you start reading in your own ideas.

If this description sounds familiar, you might want to check your reading speed. To check your speed, time yourself while you read for exactly five minutes. Estimate the total words you've read and divide by five. To estimate the total words you read, count the number of words in five lines and divide by five to get the average number of words per line. Then count the number of lines you read and multiply by the number of words per line.

For textbook material, an efficient reading speed is about 350 to 400 words per minute — depending on the difficulty of the topic and your familiarity with it. For novels and other leisure reading, many students can read 600 to 800 words per minute and "speed readers" can read much faster. Remember that understanding and flexibility in your reading style is more important than mere speed. But, often, increased speed actually improves your understanding.

You can increase your reading speed to some extent by conscious effort. If you watch someone read, you'll notice that their eyes move in "jerks" across the line. Our eyes can read words only when stopped. We read a group of words, move our eyes, read the next group, and so on. To increase reading speed, try to take in more words with each eye stop. Don't be concerned with every "and" or "but". Try to notice only words that carry meaning. Read for ideas, not words.

If you read very slowly, you should consider seeking special help. Most campuses have reading laboratories where you can get help in increasing your reading speed. Ask your instructor or advisor if your school offers such help.

Analyzing Tests

Perhaps you studied hard but still did poorly on the test. How can you make sure the same thing doesn't happen again?

You'll find it helpful to analyze what went wrong on each question you missed. You may be able to do this in class or you may need to see your instructor individually.

Compare the test and your study notes or Study Guide answers. Examine each question you got wrong and reconstruct what happened. For example, did you have the answer in your notes? If so, why didn't you recognize it on the test? Do this for each question you got wrong and look for a pattern. Here are some possibilities.

Was the answer not in your study notes at all? Perhaps you didn't answer all of a study question or, otherwise, missed important concepts. Perhaps you should talk to your instructor about his or her orientation to the course. What concepts or areas does he or she consider important? What does the instructor want you to learn? Ask the instructor to review your notes and point out where you omitted things he or she considers important.

If your study notes seem complete, go back and compare them to the text. Perhaps you misread the text, got the concept wrong, or only got part of it. Make sure you read the entire section of the text. Sometimes the first sentence of a paragraph only *seems* to convey the idea. Later sentences (or paragraphs) may really convey the core theme. Perhaps, also, you need to read faster. Slow readers often have trouble with complex concepts that aren't clearly stated in one sentence.

Perhaps the answer was in your study notes but you didn't remember it on the test. You can be pleased that you had it in your notes — but why didn't you remember it? Were you too tense? Do you need to recite and review more?

Perhaps you knew the answer but didn't recognize it because of the way the question was phrased. That suggests you're stressing memorization too much. Try to review with someone else. Get them to make you explain your answers and discuss ways they would say it differently. This will help you understand ideas when they are stated differently.

More Help

Many schools have a learning lab or learning skills center where you can get individualized help. Ask your instructor what facilities your school provides.

For ideas on using this time log, see "Finding the Time," page ix.

Time Log

Date _____

Time	Doing what?	Where?	Comments
7:00 -	-	-	
7:30 -	-	-	
8:00 -	-	-	
8:30 -	-	-	
9:00 -	-	-	
9:30 -	-	-	
10:00 -	-	-	
10:30 -	-	-	
11:00 -	-	-	
11:30 -	-	-	
12:00 -	-	-	
12:30 -	-	-	
1:00 -	-	-	
1:30 -	-	-	
2:00 -	-	-	
2:30 -	-	-	
3:00 -	-	-	
3:30 -	-	-	
4:00 -	-	-	
4:30 -	-	-	
5:00 -	-	-	
5:30 -	-	-	
6:00 -	-	-	
6:30 -	-	-	
7:00 -	-	-	
7:30 -	-	-	
8:00 -	-	-	
8:30 -	-	-	
9:00 -	-	-	
9:30 -	-	-	
10:00 -	-	-	
10:30 -	-	-	
11:00 -	-	-	
11:30 -	-	-	
12:00 -	-	-	

1 Introduction: Historical and Scientific Considerations

Overview

The first five chapters cover basic ideas and issues in abnormal psychology. These chapters are the background for the rest of the text, which covers the various forms of psychopathology and related topics.

The first two chapters discuss viewpoints on the nature of psychopathology. For example, should people with psychological problems be viewed as "sick," as having "adjustment problems," or as the victims of faulty socialization or learning?

The way we view these problems becomes especially important when discussing ways of classifying and studying psychopathology, which are covered in Chapters 3, 4, and 5. For example, if we view people with these problems as being "mentally ill," then we would want to focus on the illness, developing ways to study, diagnose, and treat it. If, instead, we perceive these people as having learned ineffective behaviors, then we will want to categorize and treat their behavior differently.

Chapter Summary

Chapter 1 covers three major topics:

What Is Abnormal Behavior? offers five characteristics of abnormality. None are, by themselves, adequate definitions of abnormality but, together, they provide a framework for understanding it.

The *History of Psychopathology* shows that different historical periods have emphasized one of three views concerning the causes of psychopathology: demonology (caused by evil outside forces), somatogenesis (bodily causes), or psychogenesis (psychological or mental causes). These three views have led society to view and treat disturbed individuals in very different ways.

Science: A Human Enterprise points out that science is never totally objective. It is influenced by the human beings who conduct it. Scientific research questions and data are influenced by the incomplete knowledge of scientists and by their views or assumptions about reality. These assumptions or paradigms influence the kinds of data scientists seek and the way they make sense out of what they find. Paradigms can also make it difficult for scientists to recognize phenomena that don't fit their paradigm.

To My Students

Before you plunge into this study guide, take a few minutes to understand it. After all, a study guide is a tool — and tools are most useful if you learn to use them properly.

This study guide comes out of my experience of what helps my students in abnormal psychology. It is designed to help them, and you, learn the material more effectively and efficiently.

The introductory chapter in this guide (entitled *Studying in This Course*) describes how to study effectively and provides suggestions for common study problems. Studying is a skill that can be learned. Read the introductory chapter for ideas on how to improve your own study skills.

For each chapter of the text, begin by reading the *Overview, Chapter Summary,* and *Essential Concepts* sections in this guide. These sections provide a broad outline of the chapter and how it fits into the overall text. That information will improve your studying later by helping you see how various details are part of broader topics.

The *Key Terms* section lists new technical terms introduced in the chapter. There is space for you to write in definitions, which is an excellent way for you to learn and study these terms.

The *Study Questions* provide a guide for studying the chapter by identifying the important ideas in each part. Read the first question, then study the indicated pages looking for the answer. Write notes on the answers you find in the space provided. Review these notes later for tests.

The *Self-Test* provides multiple-choice and short-answer questions you can use to test your knowledge.

Finally the *Visual Summary* provides a graphic review of the chapter's key concepts and their relationships.

I hope you will enjoy and benefit from your study of abnormal psychology and this study guide. I welcome your comments, criticisms, and suggestions. Please feel free to write me at the location on the title page.

Essential Concepts

1. Abnormality can be characterized in various ways. None of the characteristics hold up perfectly but, together, they provide a framework for understanding abnormality.

2. Throughout history there have been differing views on the cause of abnormal behavior. Generally abnormal behavior has been attributed to outside forces (demonology), bodily factors (somatogenesis), or mental factors (psychogenesis).

3. Contemporary views are based largely on the somatogenic and the psychogenic viewpoints.

4. The way different societies understand abnormal behavior strongly affects the way they treat it.

5. Past methods of treating abnormal behavior have varied and, often, been inhuman. However, they may not have been as bad as portrayed nor are current practices as enlightened as sometimes depicted.

6. Although science strives to be objective, it is influenced by the limited knowledge and the subjective views of scientists.

7. Paradigms or subjective assumptions are inevitable in any science. They influence what data scientists seek and what questions they ask.

Key Terms

Psychopathology (p. 3)

Abnormal behavior (p. 3)

Normal [or bell-shaped] curve (p. 4)

Demonology (p. 6)

Exorcism (p. 6)

Somatogenesis (p. 7)

Psychogenesis (p. 7)

Asylums (p. 9)

Moral treatment (p. 11)

Syndrome (p. 12)

Milieu Therapy (p. 13)

General Paresis (p. 13)

Germ theory [of disease] (p. 14)

Cathartic method (p. 15)

Clinicians (p. 16)

Clinical psychologist (p. 16)

Diagnosis (p. 16)

Psychotherapy (p. 16)

Counseling psychology (p. 16)

Psychiatrist (p. 16)

Psychoactive drugs (p. 16)

Psychoanalyst (p. 16)

Social worker (p. 16)

Psychopathologists (p. 16)

Paradigm (p. 17)

Study Questions

What is Abnormal Behavior? (p. 3–6)

1. Briefly describe five characteristics of abnormality. Explain the strengths and weaknesses of each in defining abnormality. Explain how these characteristics, collectively, form a framework for understanding abnormality. (p. 3–6)

History of Psychopathology (p. 6–15)

2.   Describe demonology and somatogenesis as early theories of the causes of deviant behavior. How did each explain abnormality?   What kinds of treatment resulted from these explanations? (p. 6–7)

3.   According to many historians, how did views and treatment of mental illness change during the Dark Ages and change again starting in the thirteenth century? What evidence suggests that the mentally ill were considered witches — and what evidence suggests they were not? (p. 7–9)

4.   Describe the development of asylums for the mentally ill during the fifteenth and sixteenth centuries. How were the mentally ill treated in these early asylums? (p. 9–10)

5.   Describe the development of moral treatment under Pinel and others. How did this approach view and treat mental illness? Why was this approach largely abandoned? (p. 10–11)

6.   Describe the development of contemporary views of somatogenesis and psychogenesis. Include the contributions of Kraepelin, Pasteur, Mesmer, Charcot, and Breuer. (p. 11–15)

Science: A Human Enterprise (p. 15–18)

7.   Identify an advantage and a disadvantage of the fact that science is conducted by human beings. (p. 15–16)

8.   Science is also limited by the subjectivity of scientists. Explain this by defining paradigms and their role in science. Why are paradigms (a) necessary and (b) potentially limiting for scientists? (p. 17)

9.   Describe the work of Langer and Abelson (1974) as an example of paradigms in abnormal psychology. How does their study illustrate the role of paradigms? (p. 17–18)

Self-test, Chapter 1

(* Items not covered in Study Questions.)

Multiple-choice

* 1. The study of psychopathology deals most directly with
      a. the development of asylums.
      b. the theories and treatments developed by followers of Freud.
      c. the nature and development of mental disorders.
      d. theories derived from animal laboratories.

2. After the death of her best friends' goldfish eight months ago, Lisa feels sad all of the time and cries herself to sleep. This example *best* illustrates which definition of abnormal behavior?
      a. Violation of norms
      b. Disability
      c. Unexpectedness
      d. Statistical infrequency

3. Hippocrates influenced psychology by
      a. distinguishing medicine from religion.
      b. emphasizing a psychogenic hypothesis of mental illness.
      c. reforming mental hospitals.
      d. suggesting mental illness was punishment from God.

4. Dorothea Dix is famous for
      a. improving hospitalized care of people with mental illness.
      b. overseeing the start of over thirty private hospitals for the mentally ill.
      c. providing moral treatment to many people with mental illness.
      d. all of the above.

* 5. Milieu therapy in modern mental hospitals involves
      a. a controlled environment wherein the effects of medication may be observed.
      b. intensive individual psychotherapy.
      c. setting up the entire hospital as a therapeutic community.
      d. regular family involvement.

6. When a group of symptoms typically co-occur, they are called
      a. syndromes.
      b. mental disorders.
      c. diagnoses.
      d. clusters.

7. The discovery of the cause of syphilis was important to the field of mental illness for which reason?
      a. Syphilis was widely feared, and exacerbated mental illness.
      b. It increased interest in determining biological causes for mental illness.
      c. More asylum patients were diagnosed with syphilis.
      d. It highlighted the need for valid diagnostic systems.

8.   Psychogenesis developed from attempts at treating which condition?
     a. demonic possession
     b. depression
     c. hysteria
     d. aphasia

* 9. Psychiatrists differ from clinical psychologists in that psychiatrists
     a. receive training in scientific bases of behavior.
     b. receive training in diagnosis of psychopathology.
     c. undergo personal analysis as part of their training.
     d. prescribe medication.

10. Paradigms in the study of abnormal behavior
     a. increase objectivity.
     b. slow innovation.
     c. increase the confidence in our conclusions regarding mental illness.
     d. enable us to gather knowledge in a systematic manner.

Short Answer

1.   What is a limitation of defining abnormality as violation of norms?

2.   What kinds of treatments evolved from early demonology?

3.   How did views on the cause of mental illness change between the Dark Ages and the 13th century?

4.   What evidence suggests that most "witches" were *not* mentally ill?

5.   How were the mentally ill treated in early asylums?

6.   Why was moral treatment largely abandoned?

7.   What is an advantage of the fact that science is conducted by human beings?

8.   In what way is science (a) objective and (b) subjective?

9.   Langer and Abelson's study illustrates the role of paradigms in psychology. Describe what they did.

10.   In what way did Langer and Abelson's research illustrate the role of paradigms?

Answers to Self-test, Chapter 1

Multiple-choice

1. c (p. 3)   2. c (p. 5)   3. a (p. 7)   4. a (p. 11)
5. c (p. 13)   6. a (p. 12)   7. b (p. 14)   8. c (p. 14)
9. d (p. 16)   10. d (p. 17)

Short Answer

1.   People with some problems (like anxiety) do not appear different (i.e. do not violate norms). Others (like criminals) violate norms but are not considered "crazy". Also norms vary across cultures. (p. 4)

2.   Attempts to induce the demons to leave through prayer, drive them out through torture, etc. (p. 6)

3.   Changed from viewing mentally ill as passively afflicted by the devil to their being actively in league with the devil. (p. 5–6)

4.   The apparent "hallucinations" of witches were extracted under torture. Government and hospitals recognized and provided for the mentally ill. (p. 8–9)

5.   Confined with lepers and social outcasts under poor conditions. Some asylums sold tickets to people who found their behavior amusing. (p. 9–10)

6.   Public hospitals became too large to provide individual care. Physicians gained control and shifted focus to biological factors. (p. 11)

7.   Science can benefit from their human ingenuity, scholarship, creativity, understanding, etc. (p. 16)

8.   Objective in the observation and collection of data. Subjective in that observations are organized based on subjective paradigms. (p. 17)

9.   Behavioral and psychoanalytic therapists viewed a videotape of a man described as either a job applicant or a patient. Then they rated the man's mental health. (p. 17–18)

10.   The two groups of clinicians saw the same tape but, because of their paradigms, reached different conclusions. (p. 18)

2 Current Paradigms in Psychopathology and Therapy

Overview

This is the second of five introductory chapters covering topics that are basic to the rest of the text. Chapter 1 discussed the role of paradigms in science generally and traced the paradigms that have been important in the history of psychopathology. Many of the differences underlying those paradigms are still unresolved. In particular, the relationship between physical and psychological factors in pathology is still widely debated. As the field has developed, other distinctions have also emerged. These distinctions underlie the current paradigms that are described in Chapter 2. These current paradigms will be used to help understand and study the various types of psychopathology described later in the text.

Chapters 3 and 4 will deal with the topics of classification and assessment. They describe the current categories of psychopathology and the methods used to assess individuals who may have psychological problems. There are a number of issues and controversies involved in both classifying pathology and assessing individuals. Not surprisingly these reflect differences among the various paradigms presented in Chapters 1 and 2.

Chapter 5 will discuss research methods in psychopathology. Then the text will begin covering the major forms of abnormality.

Chapter Summary

Chapter 2 describes five current paradigms: the biological, psychoanalytic, humanistic/existential, learning, and cognitive paradigms. Each paradigm is a viewpoint or set of assumptions about how to understand, study, and treat psychopathology.

The Biological Paradigm assumes that psychopathology, like medical disease, results from organic factors. It has led to research into behavior genetics and brain biochemistry. Biological treatments may have little relation to knowledge about biological factors in the disorder. This paradigm can also lead to reductionistic distortions.

The Psychoanalytic Paradigm originated with Sigmund Freud who looked for psychological origins of psychopathology in repressed or unconscious processes originating in childhood conflicts. Psychoanalytic techniques help lift the repression so that, as adults, we can face and handle the conflicts. Neo-Freudian analysts have shifted the emphasis from Freud's drive-based views and developed briefer therapies. Although criticized, Freud's insights underlie many contemporary ideas in abnormal psychology.

Humanistic and Existential Paradigms also promote insight but focus on understanding each unique individual and on the choices each individual can and must make in life. Humanistic therapy assumes people will make good, growth-enhancing choices when they feel accepted and valued. Existential therapy stresses, more, the inherent anxiety of making choices and accepting their consequences. Gestalt therapy fosters awareness of the immediate here-and-now in which choices are, inevitably, made.

Learning Paradigms reject mentalistic approaches and view psychopathology as ineffective behavior acquired through principles of classical conditioning, operant conditioning, and modeling. Mediational approaches extend learning principles to internal processes such as anxiety. These approaches have led to more precise methods of studying pathology and to improved treatments.

The Cognitive Paradigm considers a more complex view of learning, emphasizing that individuals actively integrate and interpret new experiences in terms of their existing understandings. Psychopathology is viewed in terms of ineffective understandings or irrational beliefs that may be relearned. This paradigm has led to popular, effective treatment methods. Cognitive therapists share many beliefs and techniques with behavioral therapists.

The *Consequences of Adopting a Paradigm* are to both focus and limit the search for answers. *Diathesis-stress: An Integrative Paradigm* may help integrate various viewpoints by considering multiple physical and psychological predispositions (diatheses) to react abnormally to particular environmental stress. *Different Perspectives on a Clinical Problem* illustrates how the same problem can make sense from a variety of paradigms. *Eclecticism in Psychotherapy* is common as therapists adjust their treatments based on a variety of paradigms.

Essential Concepts

1. Currently five major paradigms (sets of assumptions) are popular ways of understanding psychopathology. Each paradigm has evolved characteristic terminology, research, and therapeutic approaches.

2. The biological paradigm assumes that the roots of psychopathology are somatic or bodily in nature. This paradigm has produced extensive research on behavior genetics and brain biochemistry. Psychoactive drugs are used to alter functioning; although their use may not be based on knowledge about causes of the problem. The paradigm risks making reductionistic assumptions that behavior should be understood in terms of more "basic" or "underlying" biological factors.

3. The psychoanalytic paradigm assumes that psychopathology results from unconscious or repressed conflicts. Several variations have developed based on Freud's ideas about the structure of the mind, psychosexual stages of development, anxiety, and defenses. Psychoanalysts seek to lift repression so people can deal directly with conflicts.

4. Humanistic and existential paradigms assume that people can develop and change as they feel valued and supported. These therapists attempt to provide conditions in which clients can make their own choices.

5. Learning paradigms assert that abnormal behavior is learned much as normal behavior is learned. Three major learning processes have emerged: classical conditioning, operant conditioning, and mediational learning. These same processes can be used to change behavior.

6.   The cognitive paradigm views people as active learners who understand current experiences in relation to their existing cognitions. Ineffective cognitions can lead to pathology. The learning and cognitive paradigms often overlap in practice.

7.   The diathesis-stress paradigm is an attempt to integrate these paradigms account for abnormal behavior.

8.   In practice, most therapists are eclectic, blending elements from various paradigms to individualize treatment.

To My Students

I urge you to pay particular attention to this chapter.

The paradigms in Chapter 2 are a framework for much of the rest of the text. Recall that any paradigm consists of assumptions leading to particular methods of research and theorizing. Thus each paradigm has its own methods, terminology, and approaches to treatment. The paradigms in Chapter 2 (including assumptions, methods, and terms) will be used in discussing the various forms of abnormality presented throughout the text. By getting a clear understanding of each paradigm now, you'll find it much easier to make sense of the more detailed discussions later.

In addition, these are present-day paradigms. Try to identify which of them best fits your own personal paradigm (assumptions) about abnormality. This will help you recognize and evaluate your own inclinations throughout the course.

Key Terms

Biological paradigm (p. 21)

Medical [or disease] model (p. 21)

Genes (p. 21)

Behavior genetics (p. 21)

Genotype (p. 21)

Phenotype (p. 21)

Family method (p. 22)

Index cases [probands] (p. 22)

Twin method (p. 22)

Monozygotic [MZ] twins (p. 22)

Dizygotic [DZ] twins (p. 22)

Concordance (p. 22)

Adoptees method (p. 23)

Linkage analysis (p. 23)

Neuron (p. 23)

Nerve impulse (p. 23)

Synapse (p. 23)

Neurotransmitters (p. 23)

Reuptake (p. 24)

Reductionism (p. 25)

Psychoanalytic [or psychodynamic] paradigm (p. 26)

Id (p. 26)

Libido (p. 26)

Unconscious (p. 26)

Pleasure principle (p. 26)

Primary process (p. 26)

Ego (p. 26)

Secondary process (p. 26)

Reality principle (p. 26)

Superego (p. 27)

Psychodynamics (p. 27)

Psychosexual stages (p. 27)

Oral stage (p. 27)

Anal stage (p. 27)

Phallic stage (p. 27)

Latency period (p. 27)

Genital stage (p. 27)

Fixation (p. 27)

Oedipus complex (p. 27)

Electra complex (p. 27)

Objective [realistic] anxiety (p. 28)

Neurotic anxiety (p. 28)

Defense mechanism (p. 28)

Repression (p. 28)

Denial (p. 28)

Projection (p. 28)

Displacement (p. 28)

Reaction formation (p. 29)

Regression (p. 29)

Rationalization (p. 29)

Sublimation (p. 29)

Analytical psychology (p. 30)

Collective unconscious (p. 30)

Individual psychology (p. 31)

Free association (p. 31)

Resistances (p. 31)

Dream analysis (p. 31)

Psychotherapy (p. 32)

Insight therapies (p. 32)

Action therapies (p. 32)

Transference (p. 32)

Countertransference (p. 33)

Interpretation (p. 33)

Ego analysis (p. 34)

Brief therapy (p. 34)

Interpersonal therapy (p. 35)

Humanistic and existential therapies (p. 37)

Client-centered therapy (p. 37)

Self-actualization (p. 38)

Unconditional positive regard (p. 38)

Primary empathy (p. 38)

Advanced empathy (p. 38)

Gestalt therapy (p. 40)

Learning paradigm (p. 43)

Introspection (p. 44)

Behaviorism (p. 44)

Classical conditioning (p. 44)

Unconditioned stimulus [UCS] (p. 44)

Unconditioned response [UCR] (p. 44)

Conditioned stimulus [CS] (p. 44)

Conditioned response [CR] (p. 44)

Extinction (p. 44)

Law of effect (p. 45)

Instrumental learning (p. 45)

Operant conditioning (p. 45)

Discriminative stimulus (p. 45)

Positive reinforcement (p. 45)

Negative reinforcement (p. 45)

Shaping (p. 46)

Successive approximations (p. 46)

Modeling (p. 46)

Mediational theory of learning (p. 47)

Mediator (p. 47)

Avoidance conditioning (p. 47)

Behavior therapy (p. 47)

Behavior modification (p. 47)

Counterconditioning (p. 48)

Systematic desensitization (p. 48)

Aversive conditioning (p. 50)

Time out (p. 50)

Token economy (p. 50)

Role playing (p. 51)

Behavior rehearsal (p. 51)

Assertion training (p. 52)

Cognition (p. 52)

Cognitive paradigm (p. 52)

Schema (p. 53)

Cognitive behavior therapy (p. 54)

Cognitive restructuring (p. 54)

Irrational beliefs (p. 54)

Rational-emotive behavior therapy (REBT) (p. 55)

Self-efficacy (p. 57)

Diathesis-stress (p. 58)

Eclecticism (p. 61)

Study Questions

The Biological Paradigm (p. 21–26)

1.   What are the assumptions of the biological paradigm? Describe the behavior genetics view of the relationship between genes and abnormal behavior. Describe four research methods in behavior genetics and any limitations of each. (p. 21–23)

2.   Describe the biochemistry of the nervous system, especially neurotransmitters. Identify three neurotransmitter problems (amount, deactivation, receptors) that could be linked to psychopathology. (p. 23–24)

3.   Briefly describe three relationships between treatment and knowledge that a disorder has biological causes. Evaluate the biological paradigm by defining reductionism and the problem with it. (p. 24–25)

The Psychoanalytic Paradigm (p. 26–37)

4. What is the central assumption of the psychoanalytic paradigm? Briefly describe Freud's classical theory including, three mental functions, how they interact, and four (or five) stages of psychosexual development. (p. 26–28)

5. How does neurotic anxiety develop according to Freud's earlier and later theories? (Pay attention to what is repressed in each theory.) How do defense mechanisms minimize anxiety — and indicate it exists? How did Freud's changing views on childhood relationships influence his theory? (p. 28–30)

6. The text summarizes two Neo-Freudian theorists. In what way did they continue Freud's tradition? Describe about three new concepts developed by each theorist. (p. 30–31)

7.   According to psychoanalytic therapy, what can happen once repression is lifted? Describe four techniques and how each helps in reaching the goal of lifting repression. (p. 31–34)

8.   Identify three modifications of psychoanalytic therapy. Describe the major assumption of each and how therapy methods changed as a result. Evaluate the psychoanalytic paradigm by identifying four criticisms and four contributions. (p. 34–37)

Humanistic and Existential Paradigms (p. 37–43)

9.   How are humanistic and existential paradigms similar to and different from psychoanalytic paradigms? Describe five assumptions underlying Carl Rogers' client-centered therapy. Describe three characteristics of Rogers' therapeutic intervention. (p. 37–39)

10. Describe three attitudes of existential therapists (look for (a) uncertainties of life, (b) anxiety and choice, (c) accepting responsibility). Describe two goals of existential therapy. Describe the basic goal of gestalt therapy. Describe five gestalt techniques and how each can help reach the basic goal. (p. 39–42)

11. Evaluate humanistic-existential paradigms by describing (a) three criticisms and (b) research on client-centered therapy. (p. 43)

Learning Paradigms (p. 43–52)

12. How did dissatisfaction with introspection lead to the rise of the learning paradigm? What are the assumptions of behaviorism as developed by Watson and others? Describe three conditioning models (classical, operant, and modeling) which developed from behavioral assumptions. How did mediational learning paradigms modify behavioral assumptions? How did this modification expand the field? (p. 43–47)

13.   Behavior therapy is characterized by what general approach?   Briefly describe two examples of behavior therapies that developed out of each of the three conditioning models (six therapies in all). Evaluate learning paradigms by describing three issues. (p. 47–52)

The Cognitive Paradigm (p. 52–57)

14.   What is the basic assumption of the cognitive paradigm (especially that cognition is "active")? How does past knowledge influence learning of new information? Describe the cognitive behavior therapy approaches of Beck and of Ellis. Evaluate the cognitive paradigm by discussing two basic issues. (p. 52–57)

Consequences of Adopting a Paradigm/Eclecticism (p. 58–61)

15.   How do paradigms have consequences for the ways researchers collect and interpret data — and for the arguments that can result? Describe the diathesis-stress paradigm as a way to make current paradigms more flexible. What are three key points of this approach? Finally, what does it mean to say that eclecticism in psychotherapy is common? (p. 58–61)

Self-test, Chapter 2

(* Items not covered in the Study Questions.)

Multiple-choice

1. Neurotransmitters
   a. deliver nerve impulse information across the synapse.
   b. allow for the detection of brain activity, through measures such as EEG.
   c. transmit genetic information from parents to offspring.
   d. block the flow of information and contribute to behavioral problems.

2. The superego allows us to
   a. be capable of rational thought.
   b. know right from wrong.
   c. act in line with reality.
   d. be spontaneous.

3. Defense mechanisms aid in
   a. protecting the ego from anxiety.
   b. the ego expressing anxiety.
   c. preventing the superego from becoming dominant.
   d. relaxation.

*4. You seek out treatment for difficulties in coping with stress. The therapist you see focuses on resolving unconscious conflicts. You are receiving
   a. an action therapy.
   b. an insight therapy.
   c. a placebo.
   d. All of these are correct.

5. You begin to regard your therapist in a similar way to a family member. This is referred to as
   a. countertransference.
   b. identification.
   c. transference.
   d. projection.

6. As part of a session of Gestalt Therapy, Gail is asked to speak to the chair and imagine that her father is seated there. This is called
   a. role playing.
   b. empty chair technique.
   c. free association.
   d. metaphor.

7. Martha was trained in relaxation methods, and then practiced imagining feared situations while relaxed. This illustrates
   a. in vivo exposure.
   b. biofeedback.
   c. systematic desensitization.
   d. imaginal exposure.

8. Which paradigm argues that people interpret events selectively, and experience emotions based upon those interpretations?
    a. psychoanalytic paradigm
    b. cognitive paradigm
    c. learning paradigm
    d. diathesis-stress paradigm

9. When one chooses a paradigm to understand abnormal behavior, it
    a. has little effect on clinical practice.
    b. leads to an overly narrow perspective.
    c. is generally too broad in focus.
    d. aids in organizing one's conceptualization of defining, examining, and treating abnormal behavior.

10. Contemporary psychologists primarily consider themselves
    a. eclectic.
    b. psychoanalytic or psychodynamic therapists.
    c. behavior therapists.
    d. cognitive or cognitive-behavior therapists.

Short Answer

1. According to behavioral genetics, what is the relationship between genes and abnormal behavior?

2. Define reductionism.

3. What is contained in the collective unconscious according to Jung?

4. Identify four lasting contributions of Freud and psychoanalysis.

5. Identify a similarity and a difference between psychoanalysis and humanistic/existential paradigms.

6. Summarize the existential view about "choices" in people's lives.

7.   Give three criticisms of humanistic approaches to therapy.

8.   What limitation of behavioral approaches led to the development of mediational paradigms?

9.   Behavior therapy is distinguished by what general approach to abnormality?

10.   How would a therapist using Ellis' cognitive therapy approach deal with a college student who is extremely anxious about grades?

Answers to Self-test, Chapter 2

Multiple-choice

1. a (p. 23)   2. b (p. 26)   3. a (p. 28)   4. b (p. 32)
5. c (p. 33)   6. b (p. 39–40)   7. c (p. 48)   8. b (p. 52–53)
9. d (p. 58)   10. a (p. 61–62)

Short Answer

1. Phenotypes (or observable behavior characteristics) result from interaction of environment and genotypes (unobservable, genetic influences). (p. 21)

2. Reductionism is the idea that things can or should be reduced to more basic elements. For example, that behavior should be understood in terms of brain activity. (p. 25)

3. The understandings of our ancestors; experiences of humanity over the centuries. (p. 30)

4. Importance of (a) childhood, (b) unconscious influences on behavior, (c) defense mechanisms, (d) non-obvious factors in behavior. (p. 36–37)

5. Similar in emphasis on insight and awareness. Different in seeing human nature as asocial urges needing restraint versus making choices, goodness, and growth. (p. 37)

6. Living involves anxiety-provoking choices. Growth comes from facing the anxiety and making the choices. (p. 40)

7. Unclear that therapist can ever truly understand client's phenomenological world. Unclear that people are really good and able to solve own problems. Ignore possibility that people may need skills as well as insight to make changes. (p. 43)

8. Strict behavioral approaches could not easily explain situations (such as modeling) in which behavior changes without overt responding or reinforcement. (p. 46–47)

9. Epistemological stance of seeking rigorous proof. Application of experimental methods and knowledge to change abnormality. (p. 47)

10. Would suspect student has irrational beliefs such as "If I don't get As it will be terrible." or, more generally, believes one "should" or "must" get As (rather than "wanting to" get As). (p. 55)

3 Classification and Diagnosis

Overview

This is the third of five introductory chapters. The first two chapters covered historical and contemporary paradigms or theories of abnormality. The remaining three chapters deal with less theoretical issues. Chapter 3 summarizes the standard diagnostic system for classifying disturbed individuals. It also discusses some basic issues regarding classification. Chapter 4 deals with issues and methods of assessment. Mental health professionals use these methods for both individual assessment and research. Chapter 5 will cover research methods and will complete the introductory chapters.

Chapters 3, 4, and 5 are less overtly theoretical than the earlier chapters. Still, the paradigm differences continue and are reflected in differences about how best to classify and study abnormality.

Chapter Summary

Chapter 3 discusses the standard system for categorizing psychopathology and issues concerning this system as well as classification generally.

A Brief History of Classification describes early attempts to categorize abnormality and their development into the current system.

The Diagnostic System of the American Psychiatric Association (DSM-IV-TR) summarizes some general characteristics of the current standard diagnostic system, especially its multiaxial classification approach. The chapter summarizes the main categories in DSM-IV-TR. Later chapters will cover these categories in detail.

Issues in the Classification of Abnormal Behavior are (1) whether people should be classified at all and, (2) whether DSM-IV-TR is a good classification system. In classifying, we lose information and may stigmatize people. However, some classification system is needed in order to study and treat problems. Earlier DSM systems were criticized for lack of reliability (consistency in applying labels) and validity (accuracy of the labels). DSM-IV-TR appears more reliable but its broader utility is not yet clear.

To My Students

The disorders discussed in the text (beginning with Chapter 6) are primarily organized according to the classification system presented in Chapter 3. Study Chapter 3 carefully as it provides an overview of the labels and issues you will encounter later in the text.

Essential Concepts

1. Early classification systems did not clearly define disorders and were not widely accepted. Recent DSMs have provided extensive descriptions and clear reasons for label changes leading to wider acceptance.

2. The organization of mental disorders in the current Diagnostic and Statistical Manual, Fourth Edition (DSM-IV-TR) is the basis for organizing much of the text.

3. DSM-IV-TR is multiaxial, inviting consideration of five axes or dimensions when making a diagnosis.

4. In DSM-IV-TR problems are classified in sixteen major categories which are defined in this chapter.

5. Some critics object to the very concept of classifying abnormal behavior as we lose information and may stigmatize people. However, some system of distinguishing different problems seems needed.

6. The DSM approach has been criticized for using discrete categories rather than dimensions or degrees of abnormality.

7. Earlier DSMs were criticized for low reliability (consistency of diagnosis) which limited their validity or accuracy.

8. DSM-IV-TR contains specific diagnostic criteria and, as a result, has proven more reliable than its predecessors. However, its validity is uncertain and other problems remain.

Key Terms

Diagnostic and Statistical Manual of Mental Disorders (DSM) (p. 63)

Multiaxial classification (p. 65)

Disorders usually first diagnosed in infancy, childhood, or adolescence (p. 67)

Substance-related disorders (p. 67)

Schizophrenia (p. 67)

Mood disorders (p. 67)

Anxiety disorders (p. 68)

Somatoform disorders (p. 69)

Dissociative disorders (p. 70)

Sexual and gender identity disorders (p. 70)

Sleep disorders (p. 70)

Eating disorders (p. 70)

Factitious disorders (p. 70)

Adjustment disorders (p. 70)

Impulse control disorders (p. 71)

Personality disorders (p. 71)

Other conditions that may be the focus of clinical attention (p. 71)

Delirium, dementia, amnestic, and other cognitive disorders (p. 72)

Categorical classification (p. 74)

Dimensional classification (p. 74)

Reliability (p. 75)

Interrater reliability (p. 75)

Construct validity (p. 75)

Study Questions

A Brief History of Classification (p. 63–65)

1. What developments in other fields led to early interest in classifying abnormality? What was the problem with early classification systems? Identify two ways in which DSM systems addressed this problem. (p. 63–65)

The Diagnostic System of the American Psychiatric Association (DSM-IV-TR) (p. 65–72)

2. What are the five axes in DSM-IV-TR and the rationale for distinguishing them (especially axes I and II)? (p. 65)

3.   Identify and define the major diagnostic categories involved in axes I and II (16 in all). (You may wish to refer to the glossary in the back of the text.) (p. 65–72)

Issues in the Classification of Abnormal Behavior (p. 72–79)

4.   Summarize two general criticisms of classification and the counter arguments to each. Despite these criticisms, what is the general value of classification and diagnosis? (p. 73–74)

5.   Briefly identify three specific criticisms of diagnosis. (p. 74–76)

6.   For the first criticism in question 5, distinguish between categorical and dimensional approaches. Give one reason that a dimensional system should be an improvement and two reasons it might not be one. (p. 74–75)

7.   Define "reliability" and "validity". Explain them as issues in a classification system such as DSM. (p. 75–76)

8.   Describe three things done to improve the reliability of recent DSMs. (p. 76)

9.   What six problems remain in the DSM system? (p. 77–78)

Self-test, Chapter 3

(* Items not covered in Study Questions.)

Multiple-choice

* 1. In 2000, the DSM-IV-TR was published
    a. to clarify issues surrounding prevalence rates, course, and etiology.
    b. to describe diagnoses in objective terms.
    c. to include response to treatment in the descriptions of diagnoses.
    d. for use by lay persons as well as professionals.

2. Axes I and II are distinguished
    a. to distinguish mood disorders from psychotic disorders.
    b. in order to allow distinctions between medical conditions and psychological conditions.
    c. to distinguish long-term disturbance from acute problems.
    d. All of the above.

3. Sheila was recently robbed and subsequently developed an acute stress disorder. She was blinded during the robbery and is now unable to find work because of her loss of sight. Using DSM-IV, how would Sheila's problems be diagnosed?
    a. Axis I: no diagnosis; Axis II: Acute Stress Disorder; Axis III: blindness
    b. Axis I: Acute Stress Disorder; Axis II: blindness
    c. Axis I: Acute Stress Disorder; Axis II: blindness; Axis III: Psychosocial and Environment Problem: robbery
    d. Axis I: Acute Stress Disorder; Axis III: blindness; Axis IV: Psychosocial and Environmental Problem: robbery

4. Carlos is a 15-year-old who was hospitalized after he attempted suicide. He is unhappy, feels guilty, and has little energy or interest in doing anything. In which DSM-IV-TR category would his problem be listed?
    a. Schizophrenia
    b. Dissociative disorders
    c. Mood disorders
    d. Somatoform disorders

5. Symptoms of which of the following categories of DSM-IV-TR disorders are most likely to be misclassified on Axis III?
    a. Schizophrenia
    b. Mood disorders
    c. Somatoform disorders
    d. Dissociative disorders

6. In the month following his divorce, Shawn became unhappy and ate so much that he gained ten pounds. In which DSM-IV-TR category would his problem be placed?
    a. Adjustment disorders
    b. Dissociative disorders
    c. Substance abuse disorders
    d. Impulse control disorders

7. Those arguing that labeling ignores the unique qualities of the individual would suggest that
   a. all diagnostic schemes should be avoided.
   b. the DSM is not the best approach to classification.
   c. classification procedures are unreliable and inaccurate.
   d. DSM criteria should be made more explicit.

8. Dr. Kline classified her patients according to hair color. Some were classified as blonde, some brunette, some red-haired. This is an example of a
   a. continuous classification.
   b. etiological classification.
   c. categorical classification.
   d. dimensional classification.

9. Suppose someone discovered that all depressed people grew up in houses painted yellow. This finding would support the _____ of the diagnosis of depression.
   a. reliability
   b. interrater reliability
   c. construct validity
   d. predictive validity

10. Despite improvements, the current DSM system can still be criticized for
    a. not allowing for professional judgments.
    b. including too wide a range of labels.
    c. minimizing the role of physiological factors.
    d. emphasizing only treatable problems.

Short Answer

1. What developments in other fields led to early interest in classifying abnormality?

2. What was the problem with early classification systems?

3. Despite problems why is it valuable to have a system for classifying abnormality?

4. What should be the advantage of a dimensional classification of abnormality?

5. Give several examples of dimensional systems for classifying people.

6. A diagnostic label is _____ if diagnosticians agree on applying it to particular individuals.

7.   Dr. Jones has just developed the new diagnostic label of "Sprangfordism". How will he demonstrate the construct validity of this label?

8.   What was done to improve the reliability of recent DSMs?

9.   Explain what is meant by the statement that changes in recent DSMs may have improved reliability but not validity.

10.   In what ways are the rules for making diagnostic decisions less than ideal in DSM-IV-TR?

Answers to Self-test, Chapter 3

Multiple-choice

1. a (p. 64)   2. c (p. 65)   3. d (p. 65–71)   4. c (p. 67–68)
5. c (p. 69–70)   6. a (p. 70)   7. a (p. 72–73)   8. c (p. 74)
9. c (p. 75–76)   10. b (p. 76–77)

Short Answer

1. Recognition that different problems require different treatments. Recognition of the value of being able to distinguish similarities and differences in general. (p. 63–64)

2. They had vague definitions and were not widely accepted. No consensus. (p. 64)

3. Some system needed in order to study abnormality: to seek knowledge about causes and treatments (which might result in improved classification). (p. 73–74)

4. Would emphasize the continuity between normal and abnormal. That people differ in the amount of a problem rather than being "sane" versus "crazy". (p. 74)

5. Examples in which people differ in the *amount or quantity of* some characteristic. For example; height, weight, grade point average, intelligence, or income. (p. 74)

6. Reliable (p. 75)

7. By showing that accurate statements can be made about people who receive the label. For example, they are different from others in their behavior, background, prognosis, response to treatment, etc. (p. 75–76)

8. Characteristics are described extensively. Cultural differences are considered. Specific criteria for making the diagnosis are defined. (p. 76)

9. The changes have resulted in more consistent labeling (reliability) but with no guarantee that the labels will result in more useful, accurate information (validity). (p. 78)

10. The rules seem arbitrary (why 3 of 6 characteristics rather than 2 or 4 of 6?). They still involve subjective judgments. (p. 77–78)

4 Clinical Assessment Procedures

Overview

This is the fourth of five introductory chapters covering basic issues in psychopathology. The first two chapters covered historical and contemporary paradigms or theories of abnormality. Chapter 3 dealt with DSM-IV-TR, the standard system for classifying abnormality, and then went on to summarize general issues regarding classification.

This chapter discusses the major methods used to assess and classify behavior as well as issues underlying these methods. Many of these issues concern the accuracy of assessment methods. Other issues involve the paradigms discussed in Chapters 1 and 2.

Chapter 5 will cover research methods and will complete the introductory chapters. Research issues have been included in earlier chapters (and will appear throughout the text). Chapter 5 brings these issues together by showing the relative strengths and limitations of various research approaches.

Chapter 6 begins eleven chapters covering the various forms of abnormality. The last two chapters will cover related topics in abnormal psychology.

Chapter Summary

Chapter 4 describes various methods and issues in assessing individuals and their problems. It discusses issues regarding the accuracy of assessments and describes methods of assessment. Not surprisingly, these methods are based on the various paradigms discussed in earlier chapters.

Reliability and Validity in Assessment describes ways of studying the reliability (or repeatability) and validity (or accuracy) of various approaches to assessment. These concepts are used in evaluating the assessment methods described in this chapter. Generally, reliability precedes validity. That is, techniques that are not reliable or repeatable cannot easily be accurate.

Psychological Assessment covers traditional assessment techniques of clinical interviews and psychological tests (including personality inventories, projective measures, and intelligence tests). It also describes assessment techniques developed out of the behavioral and cognitive paradigms.

Biological Assessment describes methods of assessing biological influences on behavior. Brain imaging and neurochemical methods examine the brain itself. Neuropsychological methods examine the effects of brain dysfunction on behavior. Psychophysiological methods examine bodily changes that accompany behavior including changes in sweating, breathing, and heart rate. Although these methods seem precise, they have difficulty accounting for how well individuals may adapt to neurological damage.

The last two sections of the chapter discuss important (and largely unanswered) issues in assessment. *Cultural Diversity and Clinical Assessment* discusses issues in assessing individuals of differing cultures. Studies suggest clinicians may misdiagnose pathology in individuals of other cultures. These studies suggest the need for great sensitivity and awareness of cultural variation.

The Consistency and Variability of Behavior reviews a basic argument over whether behavior is consistent or variable across situations. Traditional paradigms focus on personality traits leading to predictions that behavior will be consistent across situations. Behavioral paradigms and assessments suspect behavior varies with the situation.

Essential Concepts

1. Assessment methods are evaluated in terms of "reliability" and "validity". Methods must yield reliable or repeatable results before their validity or accuracy can be effectively studied.

2. Traditional psychological assessment methods include clinical interviews, personality inventories, projective techniques, and intelligence tests.

3. Clinical interviews can be useful in establishing rapport. They are often unstructured and results depend on the interviewer's skill, paradigm, etc.

4. Personality tests are standardized, structured self-report measures, but are limited by various problems of all self-report data.

5. Projective tests rely on individuals projecting their personality as they respond to ambiguous stimuli. The unstructured nature of these procedures has made them difficult to evaluate.

6. Intelligence tests predict academic potential with some success but can be misused and misinterpreted.

7. Although direct observation is the hallmark of behavioral assessment, self-report and cognitive measures are also used.

8. Biological assessment methods study the brain itself, behavioral effects of brain dysfunction, and physiological aspects of behavior. Each method has advantages but can be misinterpreted.

9. Psychologists are becoming aware of issues in assessing individuals from differing cultures. Insensitivity to cultural variation may lead to misdiagnosis.

10. Professionals continue to debate the degree to which behavior is determined by situations or by traits. This issue reflects differences between behavioral and more traditional paradigms.

Key Terms

Interrater reliability (p. 81)

Test-retest reliability (p. 81)

Alternate form reliability (p. 81)

Internal consistency reliability (p. 81)

Content validity (p. 81)

Criterion validity (p. 81)

Concurrent validity (p. 81)

Construct validity (p. 82)

Clinical interview (p. 83)

Structured interview (p. 84)

Psychological tests (p. 84)

Standardization (p. 84)

Personality inventory (p. 84)

Minnesota Multiphasic Personality Inventory [MMPI] (p. 84)

Projective test (p. 88)

Projective hypothesis (p. 88)

Rorschach inkblots (p. 88)

Thematic Apperception Test (p. 89)

Intelligence test (p. 90)

Behavioral observation (p. 92)

Self-monitoring (p. 94)

Ecological momentary assessment [EMA] (p. 94)

Reactivity [of behavior] (p. 95)

CT [or CAT] scan (p. 97)

Meninges (p. 98)

Cerebral hemispheres (p. 98)

Corpus callosum (p. 98)

Cerebral cortex (p. 98)

Gyri (p. 98)

Sulci (p. 98)

Frontal lobe (p. 98)

Parietal lobe (p. 98)

Temporal lobe (p. 98)

Occipital lobe (p. 98)

White matter (p. 98)

Nuclei (p. 98)

Ventricles (p. 98)

Diencephalon (p. 98)

Thalamus (p. 98)

Hypothalamus (p. 98)

Midbrain (p. 99)

Brain stem (p. 99)

Pons (p. 99)

Medulla oblongata (p. 99)

Reticular formation (p. 99)

Cerebellum (p. 99)

Limbic system (p. 99)

Magnetic resonance imaging [MRI] (p. 99)

Functional magnetic resonance imaging [fMRI] (p. 99)

PET scan (p. 99)

Metabolite (p. 100)

Neurologist (p. 100)

Neuropsychologist (p. 100)

Neuropsychological tests (p. 101)

Psychophysiology (p. 102)

Electrocardiogram [EKG] (p. 102)

Electrodermal responding (p. 102)

Electroencephalogram [EEG] (p. 103)

Somatic nervous system (p. 104)

Autonomic nervous system (ANS) (p. 104)

Sympathetic nervous system (p. 105)

Parasympathetic nervous system (p. 105)

Study Questions

Reliability and Validity in Assessment (p. 80–82)

1. Define reliability and validity, and how the two are related. Briefly describe four types of reliability and three types of validity. (p. 80–82)

Psychological Assessment (p. 82–97)

2.   Identify three general approaches to psychological assessment (on pages 82, 84, and 91).
     How are interviews similar to and different from normal conversation? Describe how four
     variables (paradigms, rapport, situational factors, and structure) influence clinical interview
     results. (p. 82–84)

3.   Identify three types of psychological tests (on pages 84, 88, and 90). As an example of
     personality inventories, what was the MMPI designed to do? How was it developed and
     why was it revised? Briefly discuss the issue of faking on the MMPI. (p. 84–88)

4.   What is the assumption underlying projective tests? How have they become more
     objective over the years? (p. 88–90)

5.   What are intelligence tests designed to predict? What other uses do they have? Evaluate intelligence tests in terms of criterion validity and construct validity. (p. 90–91)

6.   Distinguish between traditional and behavioral/cognitive assessment using the SORC acronym. Describe three approaches to behavioral and cognitive assessment using examples to illustrate the range of techniques. (p. 91–97)

Biological Assessment (p. 97–105)

7.   Describe, with examples, three approaches to studying nervous system functioning. Identify advantages and disadvantages of each approach. (p. 97–102)

8.   Describe, with examples, psychophysiological measurement. Identify a limitation of this approach.   As a cautionary note, give two reasons to be cautious about biological assessment procedures generally. (p. 102–105)

Cultural Diversity and Clinical Assessment (p. 105–107)

9.   What is the basic question regarding cultural diversity and clinical assessment?   Give examples of clinicians under and overpathologizing the problems of individuals from other cultures.   What position does the text take on (a) being aware of cultural differences, and (b) including cultural differences in assessment?   Identify four strategies for avoiding cultural bias in assessment. (p. 105–107)

The Consistency and Variability of Behavior (p. 107–109)

10.   Describe Mischel's (1968) position regarding the determinates of behavior and Wachtel's three counterpoints.   Summarize the debate, including flaws in studies, self-report questionnaires, and functionality of behavior. What is the text's conclusion? (p. 107–109)

Self-test, Chapter 4

(* Items not covered in Study Questions.)

Multiple-choice

*1.   Diagnosis and clinical assessment differ in that
        a. clinical assessment asks broader questions.
        b. clinical assessment criteria are more clearly defined.
        c. diagnosis establishes the cause of the problem.
        d. diagnosis can only be done by someone with medical training.

2.   Which of the following is true regarding interviewing the client?
        a. It enables one to obtain vast amounts of information.
        b. It is too subjective to be of much value in assessment.
        c. It provides the most valid information in the assessment.
        d. Behavioral clinicians consider it unnecessary, though clinicians from other paradigms
            find it useful.

3.   Which of the following was not a change made in the revised version of the MMPI?
        a. Increase racial representativeness in the norm sample.
        b. Alter the format for answering questions.
        c. Alter the norm sample to reflect the composition of the US.
        d. Altering items to make the content more current.

4.   The projective hypothesis assumes
        a. responses to highly structured tasks reveal hidden attitudes and motivations.
        b. preferences for unstructured stimuli reveal unconscious motives.
        c. unstructured stimuli provoke anxiety.
        d. responses to ambiguous stimuli are influenced by unconscious factors.

5.   Intelligence tests were originally developed for the purpose of
        a. determining which psychiatric patients could benefit from "talk" therapy.
        b. predicting which children have special academic needs.
        c. identifying gifted children.
        d. segregating people of low intelligence so they would not have children.

6.   When Liz is in the supermarket, she feels increasing anxiety, and she then says to herself
        "I just can't stand feeling this feeling". Her self-statement would be the
        a. S.
        b. O.
        c. R.
        d. C.

7.   Xavier is recording his thoughts each time he feels depressed. This is also referred to as a
        _____ assessment
        a. projective
        b. behavioral
        c. cognitive
        d. neuropsychological

*8.   It was found through a brain scan that a man had higher than normal levels of activity in his limbic system. This man probably was having difficulty with
    a. physical movement of the body.
    b. regulation of sleep and arousal.
    c. regulation of emotion.
    d. language formation.

9.   Two people that same age, Sarah and Linda, were administered the Luria-Nebraska neuropsychological test battery. Sarah graduated with a Ph.D., while Linda did not complete high school. Assuming all other factors equal, the scores they receive on the Luria-Nebraska
    a. should differ. Sarah should score higher based on education.
    b. should differ. Linda should score higher as it is not based on education.
    c. should not differ since one controls for education level.
    d. it is impossible to predict the differences.

10.   A challenge to Mischel's view of traits is
    a. the finding that individuals shape their environment for consistency.
    b. individuals generally view themselves as consistent in their behavior.
    c. that people value consistency.
    d. All of the above choices are correct.

Short Answer

1.   How are reliability and validity related?

2.   Identify one similarity and one difference between normal conversation and clinical interviews.

3.   What type of items are used in lie scales of personality inventories such as the MMPI?

4.   How have projective tests become more objective over the years?

5.   How valid are IQ tests? Explain briefly.

6.   Dr. Jones is a behavioral psychologist helping the Smiths, who are having "discipline problems" with their child. Dr. Jones would like to directly observe this behavior without having to spend several days in the Smiths' home waiting for it to occur. What can Dr. Jones do?

7.   What is an advantage of neuropsychological assessment over other biological assessment procedures such as brain imaging?

8.   In general what are the limitations of biological measures of behavior?

9.   Why can *over*sensitivity to cultural issues among clinicians be a problem?

10. In the debate over behavioral consistency what is the issue of the "functionality of behavior"?

Answers to Self-test, Chapter 4

Multiple-choice

1. a (p. 80, 82)   2. a (p. 83)   3. b (p. 84, 86–88)   4. d (p. 88)
5. b (p. 90)   6. b (p. 91–92)   7. c (p. 95–96)   8. c (p. 97, 99)
9. c (p. 100–101)   10. d (p. 108)

Short Answer

1. Reliability limits validity. A measure that is not reliable (repeatable) cannot easily be valid (accurate or correct). (p. 81)

2. Similar as both are ways of finding out about other people. Different in that interviews only seek information about one person, the interviewee, and pay attention to *how* the interviewee says things. (p. 82–83)

3. Items that people might like to endorse but cannot do honestly. (p. 88)

4. More objective, standardized scoring methods such as Exner's have been developed. (p. 89–90)

5. They are reasonably accurate measures of what psychologists consider IQ to be (a predictor of school performance) although other factors also influence test results and school success. (p. 91)

6. Have the Smiths interact with their child in the consulting room while Dr. Jones observes. (p. 92)

7. Can detect more subtle changes by looking at how the brain functions rather than changes in its structure. (p. 101)

8. Are influenced by how well a person has adjusted to damage and his or her initial abilities as well as limitations of instruments and our knowledge of brain. (p. 103–105)

9. Oversensitivity may lead clinicians to minimize the seriousness of problems by attributing them to subcultural norms. (p. 105–106)

10. Issue of whether a behavioral trait is functional (or effective) in a particular situation. Thus both traits and situational factors may be involved. (p. 109)

5 Research Methods in the Study of Abnormal Behavior

Overview

Earlier chapters have covered paradigms or theories in psychopathology (Chapters 1 and 2) and classification and assessment issues (Chapters 3 and 4). Chapter 5 discusses scientific methods and research designs in abnormal psychology.

Many research issues have already been mentioned in Chapters 1 through 4. At times it may have seemed that scientific research creates more confusion than answers. Research can be complex, at least in part because scientists are very concerned about the limitations of their approach and their methods. It is said that there is no perfect research design. Each have both strengths and limitations. Chapter 5 describes these strengths and limitations as a basis for understanding research into the various problem behaviors discussed later in the text.

Chapter 5 is the last introductory chapter. Chapter 6 is the first of eleven chapters, comprising parts two and three of the text, discussing the various specific forms of abnormality. Chapters 6 and 7 cover problems related directly or indirectly to anxiety. These disorders used to be referred to as neuroses.

Chapter Summary

Chapter 5 discusses the methods scientists use to develop systematic knowledge as a basis for developing and evaluating theories and principles.

Science and Scientific Methods discusses basic principles of science. Statements and ideas must be publicly testable and capable of being proven false. Observations must be reliable or repeatable. Theories are propositions that both result from research and generate testable ideas for further research.

The Research Methods of Abnormal Psychology include case studies, epidemiological research, correlational studies, experiments, single-subject and mixed designs. Each method has advantages and disadvantages. They vary in the kinds of data they produce and the kinds of inferences, especially about causation, which can be drawn.

The case study is an extensive description of a particular, often unusual, problem or procedure. It is difficult to develop general principles from them, but they can provide examples to disconfirm principles and generate ideas for further research.

Epidemiological research studies how an illness or characteristic is distributed across the population. Such studies can be helpful in planning treatment needs as well as suggesting possible causes for a problem.

Correlational methods measure the relationship between two (or more) variables (for example, between course grades and anxiety). They are widely used in abnormal psychology but, because they do not actually manipulate variables, it is difficult to draw conclusions about causation from them.

In experiments one (or more) independent variables are actually manipulated and the effects of the change on dependent variable(s) are studied. Experiments are preferred for studying causation. However, in abnormal psychology, many variables cannot be manipulated for practical or ethical reasons. Experiments seek internal validity by using procedures such as control groups and random assignment. External validity is difficult with any research design.

The single-subject ABAB design studies the effect on a single individual's behavior of repeatedly (a) holding back and, (b) applying some manipulation. This design can produce dramatic results although it can be difficult to generalize results to other situations.

Mixed designs combine correlational and experimental techniques by actively manipulating only some variables.

Essential Concepts

1.   Science is the pursuit of systemized knowledge through observation, although it is not purely objective and is influenced by the paradigms of the researcher and of society.

2.   In order to be considered scientific, ideas must be publicly testable, and reliable or repeatable.

3.   Scientific theories both account for data and generate hypotheses. Theoretical concepts bridge spatial and temporal relations and summarize observed relations.

4.   The case study lacks control and objectivity, but it can be useful for (a) describing unusual phenomena, (b) disconfirming supposedly universal aspects of a theory, and (c) generating hypotheses.

5.   Epidemiological research investigates the frequency and distribution of some problem or variable in the population. Such research is useful for social planning and can suggest causes of a problem.

6.   Correlational methods study the degree of association between two or more variables (for example, IQ and grades). The variables are only observed, not manipulated. Thus, directionality and third-variable problems are difficult to answer and causal inferences are risky.

7.   Statistical significance refers to a convention adopted by scientists wherein a finding is not considered to be meaningful unless the odds are less than 5 in 100 that it occurred by chance.

8.   An experiment differs from a correlational method because one of the variables is actively manipulated. When properly conducted, an experiment is a powerful tool to study causality but ethical and practical problems often limit its use in studying psychopathology.

9. The basic features of an experiment include the experimental hypothesis, independent variables, dependent variables, and experimental effects.

10. Internal validity refers to whether the results obtained can be confidently attributed to the independent variable. Internal validity is aided by control groups and random assignment to eliminate confounds. There is debate over the role of placebo controls in psychological research.

11. External validity concerns the ability to generalize results of a particular study to other situations. It is difficult to evaluate.

12. Analogue experiments are frequently used to study psychopathology but their external validity is always of concern.

13. Single-subject research can dramatically demonstrate a phenomenon in one subject although the ability to generalize is a problem.

14. Mixed designs study the effect of several variables, some of which are observed (as in correlational methods) and some of which are actually manipulated (as in the experiment).

Key Terms

Science (p. 111)

Theory (p. 112)

Case study (p. 115)

Epidemiology (p. 117)

Prevalence (p. 117)

Incidence (p. 117)

Risk factors (p. 117)

Lifetime prevalence rates (p. 117)

Correlational method (p. 118)

Correlation coefficient [r] (p. 118)

Statistical significance (p. 119)

Classificatory variables (p. 120)

Directionality problem (p. 120)

High-risk method (p. 121)

Third-variable problem (p. 121)

The experiment (p. 121)

Experimental hypothesis (p. 122)

Independent variable (p. 122)

Random assignment (p. 122)

Dependent variable (p. 122)

Experimental effect (p. 122)

Control group (p. 123)

Confounds (p. 123)

Internal validity (p. 124)

Placebo effect (p. 124)

Placebo control group (p. 125)

Double-blind procedure (p. 125)

External validity (p. 126)

Analogue experiment (p. 127)

Single-subject experimental design (p. 127)

Reversal [ABAB] design (p. 128)

Mixed design (p. 129)

Meta-analysis (p. 130)

Study Questions

Science and Scientific Methods (p. 111–114)

1.   Describe two basic requirements of any scientific approach. Identify two roles of theory. In constructing theories, what are two advantages of theoretically inferred concepts and two views on judging the legitimacy of theoretical concepts? (p. 111–114)

The Research Methods of Abnormal Psychology (p. 114–131)

2.   List six research methods of abnormal psychology (on pages 115 to 129). What is done in a case study (the first method)? Describe three ways in which case studies are useful. (p. 115–117)

3.   What is epidemiology? Describe two uses of epidemiological research in psychopathology.
      (p. 117–118)

4.   What are correlational methods and how are they different from experimental research?
      How are correlations measured and their significance evaluated? (p. 118–120)

5.   Why are correlational methods often used in studying psychopathology?   What is their
      major drawback and two reasons for it? (p. 120–121)

6.   How does the experiment overcome the drawback of correlational methods? Identify five basic features of the experimental design. How is the significance of an experimental effect determined? (p. 121–123)

7.   What is internal validity? Describe how control groups and random assignments are used to eliminate confounds and provide internal validity. (p. 123–124)

8.   In psychotherapy research, how are placebo effects viewed? How are they controlled? Describe issues in using placebo controls in psychotherapy research. (p. 124–126)

9.   What is external validity and why is it difficult to demonstrate?   What are analogue experiments?   What is an advantage and a disadvantage of using analogues in experimental designs? (p. 126–127)

10.   What is the single-subject ABAB design and how does it show that the manipulation produced the result?   What is the primary disadvantage of this design? (p. 127–129)

11.   What is a mixed design?   Give examples, explaining why they are mixed designs.   Identify an advantage and a disadvantage of mixed designs. (p. 129–131)

Self-test, Chapter 5
(* Items not covered in Study Questions.)

Multiple-choice

1. A major weakness of operationism is that
    a. it's outdated.
    b. it eliminates the generalizability of theoretical concepts.
    c. it cannot explain individual differences.
    d. it is not conducive to scientific measurement.

2. A difficulty of case studies is
    a. lack of objectivity.
    b. limited control.
    c. few cases for comparison.
    d. all of the above choices are correct.

3. Prevalence refers to
    a. the likelihood that a disorder will be found in another culture.
    b. the proportion of a population that has a disorder now.
    c. the number of people who contract a disorder in a given time period.
    d. the likelihood that a person will have a disorder given that they have a particular characteristic.

4. A risk factor may be best defined as
    a. the likelihood that a disorder will be found in another culture.
    b. the likelihood of contracting a disorder in a given time period.
    c. the proportion of a population that has a disorder now.
    d. a characteristic that increases the likelihood of developing a disorder.

5. Dr. Samuelson finds that the relation between level of hopelessness and suicide is .35, and there is a less than 5 in 100 probability that this was found by chance alone. What would be concluded about this correlation?
    a. It demonstrates that suicide attempts cause hopelessness.
    b. It is statistically significant.
    c. It is unreliable.
    d. It is valid.

6. Which of the following is *not* a classificatory variable?
    a. Presence of depression.
    b. Sex.
    c. Taking antidepressant medication.
    d. Assignment to the treatment group of a study.

7. A research team found that men who did not exercise had a higher rate of heart disease. Which of the following explanations illustrates the third-variable problem?
    a. Heart disease might make it more difficult for men to exercise.
    b. The relationship between exercise and heart disease might not be causal.
    c. Including men who smoke in the study might erase the relationship between exercise and heart disease.
    d. Smoking might cause both heart disease and reluctance to exercise.

8.   In an experiment, the control group does not receive the
      a. third variable.
      b. independent variable.
      c. dependent variable.
      d. experimental effect.

9.   Chris is suffering from a migraine headache. His mother gives him a small white pill to
      take and tells him that it is a new medication specifically for migraines. After taking the
      pill, Chris reports feeling a bit better. The pill was actually just a breath mint. This is an
      example of
      a. misdirection.
      b. malingering.
      c. the placebo effect.
      d. the hopefulness principle.

10.   Mixed designs are combinations of
      a. experiment and single-subject.
      b. correlational and analogue.
      c. analogue and case study.
      d. correlational and experimental.

Short Answer

1.   Young Sigmund Freud was amazed at the number of his clients who reported being sexually
      abused as children. He could not believe sexual abuse was that common so he developed the
      idea of the oedipal conflict. This is an example of theory building by using _____ in order
      to _____ .

2.   How does an experiment overcome limitations of correlational methods?

3.   Experiments are said to be internally valid if . . .

4.   What does it mean to say that random assignment eliminates confounds?

5.   Professor Diaz finds that females get better scores than males on his essay tests. He would
      like to prove that this happens because they give better answers — not because of sexual
      bias on his part. Describe a double-blind procedure he could use to do this.

6.   Why is it difficult to demonstrate external validity?

7.   What factors determine whether a research study is an analogue study?

8.   You hypothesize that your professor tells jokes in class because students laugh at them. Design a single-subject ABAB design to test your hypothesis.

9.   In a single-subject ABAB design, how can we be sure that the manipulation produced the result?

10.   Give an example of a mixed research design.

Answers to Self-test, Chapter 5

Multiple-choice

1. b (p. 114)   2. d (p. 115)   3. b (p. 117)   4. d (p. 117)
5. b (p. 119)   6. d (p. 120)   7. d (p. 121)   8. b (p. 123)
9. c (p. 124)   10. d (p. 129)

Short Answer

1. (using) an inferred theoretical concept (in order to) bridge spatiotemporal relations. (p. 112)

2. Variables are controlled by actual manipulation (independent variable) or by randomization (using random assignment) to eliminate directionality and third-variable problems. (p. 122).

3. The effect can be confidently attributed to manipulating the independent variable. (p. 124)

4. By randomly assigning participants to groups any individual characteristics of the participants which might influence the results (i.e. be confounds) are equally likely to occur in all groups. (p. 124)

5. Professor Diaz could have someone else, who will not be involved in grading the tests, remove all names and identifying information from the test papers before he scores them. (p. 125)

6. There is no way to know for sure to which other situations results will generalize. The best one can do is perform similar experiments in new situations. (p. 126)

7. How the results are used. What implications are made or what other situations the results are applied to. (p. 127)

8. Laugh at each joke your professor tells for one class session and don't laugh for the next session. Repeat this several times. Count the number of jokes told in each session. (p. 128)

9. By reversing (introducing and removing) the independent variable repeatedly. When the behavior repeatedly changes along with the independent variable, we can feel confident that the manipulation produced the change. (p. 128)

10. Your example should include two independent variables, one of which is simply measured (a classificatory variable) and one of which is manipulated. For example: compare test scores of male and female students (a classificatory variable) after they spend two hours hearing a lecture or reading the text (a manipulation). (p. 129)

Overview

The first five chapters have discussed a number of basic ideas and issues in abnormal psychology. These concepts provide a framework for surveying the various forms of abnormality. You will want to refer back to these chapters periodically as you study the rest of the text.

The next eleven chapters survey the various forms of abnormality. Now would be a good time to glance over all these chapters. Notice that they cover a wide range of problem behaviors. A number of them are matters of current social debate. After covering forms of abnormality, the last two chapters in the text discuss issues in intervention as well as legal and ethical issues.

The first two chapters on forms of abnormality, Chapters 6 and 7, discuss problems related directly or indirectly to anxiety. Chapter 6 covers anxiety disorders which more or less directly involve excessive fears, worries, and anxiety. Chapter 7 discusses two groups of problems where anxiety may be more subtly involved. They are somatoform disorders, characterized by physical symptoms or complaints, and dissociative disorders, involving disturbances in memory and awareness. Although the traditional psychoanalytic term "neurosis" is no longer used to describe these problems, anxiety is still seen as involved in various ways.

Chapters 8 and 9 look at other problems that also involve anxiety but in which physical and medical issues are more prominent. Chapter 8 discusses stress effects on general health as well as on psychophysiological disorders, such as ulcers and heart conditions, which have long been recognized as involving anxiety and stress. Chapter 9 focuses on eating disorders, such as anorexia nervosa, which involve health problems resulting from cultural and other stresses.

Chapter Summary

Chapter 6 begins the survey of psychological problems by discussing anxiety disorders. In studying the chapter, look for the format described in "To My Students" below. Five kinds of anxiety disorders are discussed:

Phobias are relatively common disorders involving intense, unreasonable, disruptive fears of particular situations. They include (a) specific phobias such as fear of snakes and (b) social phobias such as fear of public embarrassment. Psychoanalysts view phobias as defenses against repressed conflicts. Behaviorists have offered avoidance, modeling and prepared learning models for the development of phobias. These models, as well as cognitive and biological approaches, have led to treatment approaches.

Panic Disorder involves sudden, unexpected attacks of anxiety. Panic attacks may lead to agoraphobia or fear of leaving safe places. Research suggests that these people escalate stressors into full-blown panic due to their fear-of-fear or fear of loss of control. People with *Generalized Anxiety Disorder* live in relatively constant tension. People with *Obsessive-compulsive Disorders* are bothered by unwanted thoughts (obsessions) and/or feel compelled to engage in repetitive rituals (compulsions) lest they be overcome by anxiety. There are a variety of psychoanalytic, behavioral, cognitive, and biological views on the cause of each disorder that have led to corresponding treatments.

Posttraumatic Stress Disorder reflects a recognition that traumatic events such as disasters or combat may affect anyone. Aftereffects include reexperiencing the traumatic event, avoiding stimuli associated with the event, and increased arousal. Treatments emphasize rapid intervention, and talking through or reliving the event in a supportive atmosphere.

To My Students

This is the first of many chapters covering specific psychological disorders. As you study them you will discover that each follows the same general outline. First, the problem is defined and any issues regarding its classification in DSM-IV-TR are discussed. Second, theories and research into its causes are described. Typically these include the Psychoanalytic, Behavioral, Cognitive, and Biological paradigms. Finally, various treatments are summarized using the same paradigms. Of course the outline varies, but you will find it helpful to look for this kind of outline as you study each chapter and to organize your studying around it.

This is also a good time to warn you of a common experience among students studying abnormal psychology. Often, students in these courses come to believe they may have the problem covered in each chapter. For example, you may think you have an anxiety disorder when studying Chapter 6, depression in Chapter 10, and schizophrenia in Chapter 11. If this happens to you, don't be surprised. The various problems covered in the text are exaggerations of very normal tendencies in all of us. If you can see these tendencies in yourself, it probably means you have developed a meaningful understanding of the problem. Of course, if you are seriously concerned, you can discuss the matter with your instructor or someone at your school's counseling center. They are used to such situations and you may be surprised at how easily they understand your concerns.

Essential Concepts

1. Anxiety disorders used to be called neuroses based on the psychoanalytic view that anxiety is caused by unconscious conflict.

2. The major categories of anxiety disorders listed in DSM-IV-TR are: phobias, panic disorder, generalized anxiety disorder, obsessive-compulsive disorder, and posttraumatic stress disorder.

3. A phobia is a disrupting, fear-mediated avoidance, out of proportion to the actual danger from the object or situation that is feared.

4. Psychoanalytic, behavioral, cognitive, and biological models of phobias have been proposed. None account for all phobias. A diathesis model allows for consideration of multiple factors to account more fully for phobias.

5. Various therapies for phobias emphasize reexperiencing the feared situation. Drugs have also been used but are typically effective only so long as the person continues to take them.

6.   Panic disorders, involving unexpected attacks of anxiety, may lead to agoraphobia or fear of public places. Several biological and psychological approaches exist.

7.   Generalized anxiety disorder, characterized by chronic anxiety, has often been viewed and treated in ways similar to phobias. Treatment approaches seek to help people manage their fears in various ways.

8.   Obsessive-compulsive disorder involves obsessive thoughts and compulsive behaviors. A wide range of causes and treatments have been proposed with limited success.

9.   Posttraumatic stress disorder (PTSD) is, primarily, an aftereffect of experiencing trauma, although other factors increase the risk of PTSD after a trauma.

10.   PTSD is treated various ways. Typically treatment stresses immediate intervention, exposure under supportive conditions, and social support.

Key Terms

Anxiety (p. 133)

Neuroses (p. 134)

Anxiety disorders (p. 134)

Comorbidity (p. 134)

Phobia (p. 134)

Specific phobias (p. 136)

Social phobia (p. 136)

Vicarious learning (p. 138)

Flooding (p. 143)

Anxiolytics (p. 144)

Panic disorder (p. 145)

Depersonalization (p. 145)

Derealization (p. 145)

Agoraphobia (p. 145)

School phobia (p. 146)

Selective mutism (p. 146)

Generalized anxiety disorder [GAD] (p. 152)

Obsessive-compulsive disorder [OCD] (p. 157)

Obsessions (p. 157)

Compulsion (p. 157)

Posttraumatic stress disorder [PTSD] (p. 163)

Acute stress disorder (p. 163–164)

Study Questions

1.   Define "neuroses" pointing out the theoretical assumptions involved. How have recent DSMs dealt with this term? Describe "anxiety disorders" generally. Identify two reasons for comorbidity. (p. 134)

Phobias (p. 134–145)

2.   What are phobias and why do psychoanalysts (but not behaviorists) focus on their content? Describe two types of phobias. Summarize the Freudian theory of phobias. Summarize three behavioral theories of phobias. (p. 134–139)

3.   How would it be helpful to add the idea of "diatheses" to the behavioral theories? Describe four possible diatheses for phobias (social skills, cognitive, autonomic, genetic). (p. 139–141)

4.   Summarize the (a) psychoanalytic, (b) behavioral (five techniques), and (c) cognitive approaches to therapy for phobias. What do all these techniques have in common? What is the key problem with the common biological treatment? (p. 141–145)

Panic Disorder (p. 145–152)

5.   Describe the characteristics of panic disorder and its relation to agoraphobia. Evaluate four biological and two psychological factors or hypotheses about panic disorder. (p. 145–150)

6.   Identify one advantage and five disadvantages to biological treatments for panic disorders. Describe two general psychological treatments and compare their effectiveness to biological treatments. (p. 150–152)

Generalized Anxiety Disorder (p. 152–156)

7.   Describe the characteristics of generalized anxiety disorder. Summarize the psychoanalytic, two cognitive-behavioral, and two biological views on its cause. (p. 152–154)

8. Under therapies for generalized anxiety disorder the text summarizes one psychoanalytic, two behavioral, two cognitive, and one biological approach. Describe and evaluate the effectiveness of each. (p. 154–156

Obsessive-Compulsive Disorder (p. 156–163)

9. Define and give several examples of obsessions and of compulsions. How are these definitions different from the way we commonly use terms such as "compulsive"? Summarize views on the causes of obsessive-compulsive disorders (one psychoanalytic, five behavioral and cognitive, and three biological views). (p. 156–160)

10. How effective are treatments for OCD generally? Briefly summarize five treatments for obsessive-compulsive disorders (including two biological treatments). (p. 160–163)

Posttraumatic Stress Disorder (p. 163–171)

11. How is posttraumatic stress disorder (PTSD) defined differently from most disorders? Describe three main characteristics of PTSD. Describe risk factors for PTSD including severity of trauma, dissociative symptoms, and coping style. Describe three theories of its cause. (p. 163–166)

12. What is the basic principle in treating PTSD. Describe a total of eight approaches to treating PTSD and the scientific (or political) issues regarding each. (Look for CISD, Wartime approaches in WW II and in Vietnam, behavioral, cognitive, EMDR, psychoanalytic, and biological.) (p.166–171)

Self-test, Chapter 6
(* Items not covered in Study Questions.)

Multiple-choice

1. Margaret and Ed have different fears. Margaret is afraid of snakes, whereas Ed is afraid of dogs. Their fears are similar in that
    a. both serve the same adaptive purpose.
    b. both require aversive learning consequences for their development.
    c. neither respond well to treatment.
    d. All of the above choices are correct.

2. "This patient has a phobia of elevators because he had a frightening experience in an elevator when he was a young child". This statement would most likely be made by a clinician from the which paradigm?
    a. Biological
    b. Psychoanalytic
    c. Humanist
    d. Behavioral

3. Doug was frightened by a rat coming into his bedroom when he was a child, and he now has a rat phobia. However, despite having been severely shocked by putting her finger in an electric outlet, Martha has no fear of sockets. This inconsistency is explained by the theory of
    a. preparedness.
    b. systematic desensitization.
    c. irrational beliefs.
    d. avoidance conditioning.

4. Ego analysis of phobias is most similar to
    a. traditional psychoanalysis.
    b. interpersonal therapy.
    c. behavioral treatment, such as flooding.
    d. social skills training.

*5. School phobia in young children is most often associated with
    a. fear of being away from parents.
    b. fear of humiliation by peers.
    c. fear of academic demands.
    d. fear of the unknown.

6. Agoraphobia is characterized by a fear of
    a. being in unfamiliar places.
    b. being embarrassed by saying or doing something foolish in front of others.
    c. strangers misinterpreting their symptoms as a heart attack.
    d. having a panic attack in public.

7.   The primary goal of having clients with panic attacks experience primary symptoms of panic in the therapy room is
     a. to reinterpret physical symptoms from loss of control to harmless physical variations.
     b. to develop a clearer understanding of the role panic symptoms play in their life.
     c. the development of higher fear to be adjusted by direct therapy once the panic has been initiated.
     d. to access underlying psychodynamic features of the client.

8.   What diagnosis is most appropriate for Nicole? She is constantly concerned with symmetry, often spending hours arranging items in her room so that the room appears even on the left and right. She also feels that when she eats, the items on the plate must be arranged symmetrically. All of this effort interferes with her work.
     a. Obsessive-compulsive disorder
     b. Specific phobia
     c. Generalized anxiety disorder
     d. Specific phobia

9.   A strictly behavioral therapist treating Steve for contamination fear due to OCD would use which of the following interventions?
     a. Have Steve meditate daily.
     b. Have Steve challenge the idea it is necessary to be clean.
     c. Have Steve purposely get dirty.
     d. Have Steve say 'stop' to himself quietly when he feels he must wash.

10.   Which of the following has been shown useful in treating posttraumatic stress disorder?
     a. Training in minimizing emotional outbursts.
     b. Having the person confront their fears.
     c. Prolonged rest, peace and quiet.
     d. Firm encouragement to get on with their life.

Short Answer

1.   What assumption was the basis for the term "neurosis"?

2.   Define "social phobia," distinguishing it from specific phobias.

3.   Why does the text urge adding a diathesis to behavioral theories of phobias?

4.   Describe what is done in systematic desensitization as a treatment for phobias.

5.   In what way are panic disorder and generalized anxiety disorder similar?

6.   What is the basis for generalized anxiety according to the psychoanalytic view?

7.   Mary is chronically anxious. She is very shy and awkward around others. She reports feeling that she can't do anything right and that no one likes her. What would a behavioral therapist view her problem?

8.   What is the distinction between obsessions and compulsions?

9.   How is PTSD defined differently from most disorders?

10.   What topics were commonly discussed in rap sessions conducted to help Vietnam veterans deal with stress reactions?

Answers to Self-test, Chapter 6

Multiple-choice

1. a (p. 135)   2. d (p. 137–138)   3. a (p. 138–139)   4. c (p. 142, 144)
5. a (p. 146)   6. d (p. 145, 148)   7. a (p. 151–152)   8. a (p. 156–157)
9. c (p. 161)   10. b (p. 169–170)

Short Answer

1.   Freudian assumption that many problems were based, directly or indirectly, on repressed anxiety. (p. 134)

2.   Unreasonable fears tied to presence of others, public situations, etc. Specific phobias involve specific situations. Social phobia involves a wide range of situations. (p. 136)

3.   Because not all people develop phobias after a traumatic experience. Avoidance conditioning plus something else seems needed. (p. 139)

4.   Individual is taught how to relax deeply. Then, while relaxed, the person imagines a series of gradually more fearful situations. (p. 142)

5.   Person experiences anxiety which is *not* linked to a particular situation (i.e. not a phobia). (p. 145, 152)

6.   Conflicts and impulses that have been repressed. The individual is afraid but does not know what he or she is afraid of because it is repressed. Thus, the fear is chronic. (p. 153)

7.   Behaviorist would see her anxiety as tied to social fears (a social phobia or cued fear). (p. 154)

8.   Obsessions are thoughts and compulsions are behaviors. (p. 157)

9.   The cause or etiology is part of the definition. (p. 163)

10.   Feelings about the war (guilt, anger), about family life (social and family changes), and society's attitudes toward the war. (p. 168)

7 Somatoform and Dissociative Disorders

Overview

Chapter 7 is the second chapter on disorders related to anxiety and stress. The previous chapter discussed disorders involving fairly direct expressions of anxiety. These included chronic anxiety, phobias or unreasonable fears, and obsessions and compulsions in which people think and do things in order to control anxiety. Chapter 7 describes disorders in which people may not directly complain of anxiety but have other problems that appear related to anxiety and stress in some way. These are somatoform disorders (involving physical complaints) and dissociative disorders (involving altered memory and awareness). Both arise from psychological factors such as anxiety and stress.

After this, Chapters 8 and 9 discuss how anxiety and stress can lead to illness and physical or tissue changes. Traditionally, we have recognized the role of stress in psychophysiological disorders such as ulcers. However, we now recognize that stress can play a role in virtually all physical/medical problems. Chapter 8 discusses both these roles. Chapter 9 discusses eating disorders, such as anorexia nervosa, which also involve anxiety and physical problems. However, eating disorders also involve significant social and cultural issues.

Chapter Summary

Chapter 7 covers two groups of disorders in which there is a loss of physical function with no physical basis. The symptoms seem to serve a psychological purpose.

Somatoform Disorders are characterized by physical complaints that have no physiological basis. The text emphasizes two of these disorders. In conversion disorder there is a loss of sensory or motor functioning: for example a loss of vision, touch, etc., or of the ability to walk, talk, etc. In somatization disorder there are multiple physical complaints such as headaches, various pains, and fatigue typically involving repeated visits to physicians and medical treatment.

Knowledge about somatoform disorders is limited because individuals with these problems typically seek medical, not psychological, treatment. Existing theories deal primarily with conversions. Psychoanalysts propose that repressed conflicts are "converted" into the physical symptoms in various ways and seek to uncover what was repressed. Behavioral theorists suggest that the behaviors reduce anxiety and seek to teach more effective behaviors.

Dissociative Disorders involve problems with awareness and memory. In dissociative amnesia, the individual is unable to recall important personal information, often of traumatic events. Dissociative fugue involves a more encompassing memory loss in which the person leaves home and assumes a new identity. Depersonalization disorder is characterized by disconcerting alternations in perception of the self. In dissociative identity disorder (DID), two or more separate and distinct personalities occur in alternation, each having its own memories, behaviors, and life styles.

Psychological theories propose that memory losses in dissociative disorders protect the individual from traumatic memories, perhaps of childhood abuse. Another theory suggests they are learned social roles. Because these disorders strongly suggest repression, psychoanalytic techniques are often used in treatment.

Essential Concepts

1. Conversion disorder and somatization disorder are two major categories of somatoform disorders.

2. In conversion disorders, muscular or sensory functions are impaired with no apparent physical basis so that the symptoms seem to be linked to psychological factors.

3. It is difficult to distinguish between conversion disorder, physical illness, and malingering.

4. Somatization disorder is characterized by recurrent, multiple somatic complaints for which medical attention is sought but which have no apparent physical basis.

5. Conversion disorders occupy a historic place in psychoanalytic thinking because their nature led Freud to emphasize the unconscious. Psychoanalysis developed as a technique to overcome these repressed impulses.

6. Behaviorists suggest that conversions are reinforced and treatment focuses on teaching more effective ways to get reinforcers.

7. The dissociative disorders (dissociative amnesia, dissociative fugue, depersonalization, and dissociative identity disorder) involve disruptions of consciousness, memory, and identity.

8. The memory losses in dissociative disorders strongly suggest psychoanalytic concepts of repression. Thus, psychoanalytic techniques are widely used in treating these disorders.

Key Terms

Somatoform disorders (p. 172)

Dissociative disorders (p. 172)

Pain disorder (p. 173)

Body dysmorphic disorder (p. 173)

Hypochondriasis (p. 174)

Conversion disorder (p. 174)

Anesthesias (p. 174)

Hysteria (p. 175)

Malingering (p. 176)

La belle indifference (p. 176)

Factitious disorder (p. 176)

Somatization disorder (p. 176–177)

Dissociative amnesia (p. 186)

Dissociative fugue (p. 186)

Depersonalization disorder (p. 187)

Dissociative identity disorder [DID] (p. 187)

Study Questions

Somatoform Disorders (p. 173–185)

1.   What are the general characteristics of somatoform disorders? Describe and distinguish among three types of somatoform disorders (which are not discussed in detail.). (p. 173–174)

2. Give some examples of conversion symptoms involving loss of (a) motor, and (b) sensory functioning. Why is it difficult, but important, to distinguish between conversions and medical conditions? (p. 174–176)

3. Describe somatization disorder. How is it similar to and different from conversion disorder? What role does culture (probably) play in somatization disorder? (p. 176–177)

4. How did the study of conversions lead Freud to important concepts? Summarize Freud's early theory of conversions and his later revision of it. (p. 178–179)

5.   Summarize contemporary psychodynamic research on conversions and the resulting revision of Freud's theory. (p. 179–180)

6.   Describe three other approaches to understanding conversion disorders. How well is each supported by research? (p. 180–183)

7.   Why has little research been done on the psychological treatment of somatoform disorders? How do psychoanalysts approach somatoform disorders in general. How do cognitive-behavioral therapies approach somatization disorder, hypocondriasis and pain disorder? (p. 183–185)

Dissociative Disorders (p. 185–196)

8.   Define and distinguish among four dissociative disorders. (p. 185–188)

9.   Explain how controversy about dissociative identity disorder (or DID) has been influenced by (a) changes in prevalence, (b) confusion with schizophrenia, and (c) popular cases. (p. 188–190)

10.   Explain the general view of the mechanism underlying dissociative disorders. Describe two major theories of the cause of DID and a study supporting each. (p. 190–192)

11. Summarize general principles in the treatment of dissociative disorders as a group and dissociative identity disorder in particular. (p. 192–196)

Self-test, Chapter 7

(* Items not covered in Study Questions.)

Multiple-choice

1. William has been diagnosed with body dysmorphic disorder because of his excessive concerns about having too much body hair. Which of the following would eliminate his symptoms?
    a. Plastic surgery.
    b. Eliminating all mirrors from his house.
    c. Shaving.
    d. None of the above.

2. The onset of conversion symptoms is usually
    a. sudden and related to a stressful situation.
    b. gradual and subtle.
    c. not associated with psychological distress.
    d. preceded by a period of physical illness.

3. Sandra has 'glove anesthesia.' This diagnosis
    a. may be incorrect if Sandra has a job involving a great deal of typing.
    b. can be made with near certainty.
    c. depends on the degree of accompanying anxiety experienced by the patient.
    d. is not appropriate; pain disorder is the correct term.

* 4. Unlike a malingerer, a person with factitious disorder
    a. does not exhibit "la belle indifference".
    b. has primarily psychological, not physical, symptoms.
    c. has physical symptoms that are not under voluntary control.
    d. has no clear motivation for adopting the symptoms.

5. The psychodynamic perspective on conversion disorder was revised in light of experimental findings with hysterically blind people who
    a. have underlying brain defects.
    b. can see when under hypnosis.
    c. can respond to visual information.
    d. experienced traumatic visual events.

6. Which model has been *least* helpful in understanding conversion disorders?
    a. Psychoanalytic
    b. Behavioral
    c. Sociocultural
    d. Genetic

7. The treatment of somatoform disorders is relatively primitive because
    a. sufferers rarely seek mental health treatment.
    b. they are rare in the population.
    c. efforts to treat them have been unsuccessful.
    d. of legal and professional prohibitions.

8.   Recovery from dissociative fugue is
    a. usually sudden and complete.
    b. difficult to achieve.
    c. likely only after lengthy therapy.
    d. accomplished in brief therapy.

* 9. The most commonly diagnosed comorbid disorder with dissociative identity disorder is
    a. depression.
    b. generalized anxiety disorder.
    c. posttraumatic stress disorder.
    d. schizophrenia.

*10. Repressed memories of childhood sexual abuse are considered to be
    a. accurate.
    b. inaccurate.
    c. partially accurate.
    d. none of the above; the accuracy remains unknown.

Short Answer

1.   What are the characteristics of hypochondriasis?

2.   Distinguish between conversion disorder and somatization disorder.

3.   How did the study of conversions lead Freud to important concepts?

4.   Describe the psychodynamic studies that led to a contemporary revision of Freud's theory of conversions.

5.   Summarize a behavioral approach to the cause of conversion disorders.

6.   Describe the cognitive-behavioral approach to the treatment of hypocondriasis.

7.   Give several reasons the existence of dissociative identity disorder is disputed.

8.   What is the general view of the mechanism underlying dissociative disorders in general?

9.   Describe studies supporting the view of dissociative identity disorder as role-playing.

10.   What is the basic approach to treatment of dissociative disorders in general (not DID in particular)?

Answers to Self-test, Chapter 7

Multiple-choice

1. d (p. 173)   2. a (p. 174)   3. a (p. 175)   4. d (p. 176)
5. c (p. 179)   6. d (p. 183)   7. a (p. 183)   8. a (p. 187)
9. c (p. 193)   10. d (p. 194)

Short Answer

1.   Preoccupation with fear of having a serious medical illness. (p. 174)

2.   Conversion symptoms emphasize a loss of functioning while somatization disorder symptoms emphasize complaints about loss of functioning. The distinction can be difficult in practice. (p. 174, 177)

3.   Their existence led him to emphasize the unconscious. If medical causes and deliberate faking are ruled out, then the cause "must" be unconscious. (p. 178)

4.   Case studies in which individuals with conversions involving blindness would "guess" visual stimuli much better or worse than chance. (p. 179)

5.   The behaviors are learned. The individual may have learned (through modeling) that sick people behave this way or the behaviors may be reinforced by attention and getting out of things. (p. 180–182)

6.   Attempt to restructure pessimistic preoccupations about health issues. (p. 185)

7.   The rate of DID diagnoses has varied widely depending, seemingly, on popular writings. DID was an issue in several highly publicized trials. (p. 188–189)

8.   Traumatic memories are not remembered because they are stored differently and/or attempts to recall them are painful (i.e. punished). (p. 190)

9.   College students given a rudimentary hypnotic induction were able to manifest two different personalities in interviews and on psychological tests. (p. 191–192)

10. Generally treat using psychoanalytic principles and/or same approach as PTSD by encouraging recall of traumatic memories in a safe situation. (p. 192–193)

8 Psychophysiological Disorders and Health Psychology

Overview

The last two chapters covered psychological disorders linked to anxiety. Chapters 8 and 9 cover problems related to anxiety in more complex ways. The disorders covered in Chapters 6 and 7 were, traditionally, referred to as neuroses. Those in Chapter 6 involved more-or-less direct difficulties with anxiety. In Chapter 7 the disorders did not directly involve anxiety but, traditionally, anxiety is believed to underlie them. They were somatoform disorders (involving physical symptoms) and dissociative disorders (involving memory, consciousness, and identity). All the problems in Chapter 7 involve physical complaints without physically detectable changes in the body. In contrast, the problems covered in Chapter 8 involve physically detectable changes.

It should be clear by now that anxiety is a source of much psychological suffering. Anxiety and stress also have physical effects. Some of these, such as heart disease, ulcers, and asthma, have traditionally been termed psychophysiological disorders. However, that term has been discarded with the realization that stress is a factor in illness and health generally. Chapter 8 discusses stress and health generally as well as the psychophysiological disorders.

Chapter 9 will cover eating disorders such as anorexia nervosa. Eating disorders also involve physical problems and tissue change. They surely result from anxiety and stress, broadly defined. However, more specifically, they appear related to cultural pressures to control weight, especially among women.

After Chapter 9, the text shifts focus. Chapters 10 and 11 cover mood disorders (such as depression) and schizophrenia. These are more complex problems, at least in terms of treatment and research (especially physiological research).

Chapter Summary

Chapter 8 generally focuses on the role of psychological factors in physical illnesses. Psychological factors have been considered especially strong in medical conditions traditionally referred to as psychophysiological disorders. However, DSM dropped that term recognizing that psychological factors contribute to some degree in virtually all medical illnesses. The chapter also discusses some common examples of psychophysiological disorders in detail.

Stress and Health reviews efforts to define and measure stress and its relation to physical illness in general. *Theories of the Stress-Illness Link* identify a number of both biological and psychological theories regarding this relationship.

Cardiovascular Disorders including hypertension and heart disease appear related to specific styles of responding to stress, especially Type A behavior and cynicism/anger.

Asthma attacks involving difficulty in breathing result from combinations of psychological factors and biological predispositions that vary from individual to individual.

AIDS: [is] *A Challenge for the Behavioral Sciences* because behaviors and behavioral issues are central to its spread and to its control. With no medical cure yet available, efforts such as safe-sex education offer the best current hope of controlling the epidemic.

Sections on *Gender and Health* and *Socioeconomic Status, Ethnicity, and Health* discuss how these factors effect health and longevity. While genetic factors cannot be ruled out, differences are largely related to such factors as access to care, life styles, and stress.

Therapies for Psychophysiological Disorders involve treating current symptoms and underlying conditions using both medical and psychological approaches. Psychological approaches are used to reduce risk factors, to change general psychological contributors, and to teach specific skills. Behavioral medicine, a new specialization, is developing specialized psychological techniques to treat psychophysiological disorders and other medical conditions.

Essential Concepts

1.   Psychophysiological disorders are distinct from conversion reactions and involve physical tissue changes that are caused or worsened by emotional factors.

2.   There is no listing of psychophysiological disorders in DSM-IV-TR because virtually all physical illnesses are now viewed as potentially related to psychological factors.

3.   Stress has been defined in various ways, including stressful events, stress responses, and coping skills.

4.   A number of research approaches indicate relationships between stress and illness. Coping skills and social supports influence these relationships.

5.   There are both biological and psychological theories about the link between stress and illness.

6.   There is much research on psychological factors contributing to cardiovascular disorders and asthma.

7.   High blood pressure and coronary heart disease appear related to Type A behaviors, especially the suppression of anger, although this research is complex and ongoing.

8.   Asthma apparently results from a combination of physical and psychological factors whose importance varies with the individual.

9.   AIDS is a challenge for the behavioral sciences because, without a medical cure, psychological approaches offer the best hope of controlling the epidemic through education, etc.

10. Longevity and health vary with gender. Gender related differences in personality and life style are probably responsible though data on women is limited.

11. Health and longevity vary among socioeconomic and ethnic groups. These differences appear, at least largely, to be the result of differing access to services, lifestyles, stresses, and similar factors.

12. Where psychological factors contribute to illness, a combination of medical and psychological treatment is needed.

13. Behavioral medicine is developing specific programs for treating psychological factors that contribute to illness.

Key Terms

Psychophysiological disorders (p. 198)

Psychosomatic disorders (p. 198)

Psychological factors affecting medical condition (p. 198)

Behavioral medicine (p. 199)

Health psychology (p. 199)

Stress (p. 199)

General adaptation syndrome [GAS] (p. 199)

Stressor (p. 200)

Coping (p. 200)

Structural social support (p. 204)

Functional social support (p. 204)

Somatic-weakness theory (p. 207)

Specific reaction theory (p. 207)

Allostatic load (p. 207)

Anger-in theory (p. 209)

Cardiovascular disorders (p. 210)

Essential hypertension (p. 210)

Coronary heart disease [CHD] (p. 214)

Angina pectoris (p. 214)

Myocardial infarction (p. 214)

Type A behavior pattern (p. 215)

Asthma (p. 218)

Biofeedback (p. 233)

Community psychology (p. 234)

Stress management (p. 236)

Study Questions

1. Define psychophysiological disorders, distinguishing them from conversion disorders (in Chapter 7). How does DSM-IV-TR handle psychophysiological disorders? How does this approach lead to broader understandings of the relationship between stress and illness? (p. 198–199)

Stress and Health (p. 199–206)

2. Describe three approaches to defining stress and the limitations of each. (p. 199–201)

3. Describe two efforts to measure stress. The first study uses a retrospective approach. Why is this approach problematic and how is the second study an improvement? Describe how coping is commonly assessed. (p. 201–204)

4.   Describe two social moderators of the stress-illness link. What are some ways they may influence the relationship between stress and illness? (p. 204–206)

Theories of the Stress-Illness Link (p. 206–210)

5.   What kinds of questions are confronted by theories of the stress-illness link? Briefly describe two reasons to be cautious about all these theories. Describe four biological theories and two psychological theories. (p. 206–210)

Cardiovascular Disorders (p. 210–218)

6.   What is essential hypertension and how much of a problem is it? Describe the methods and results of (a) two ways of studying the relation between psychological stress and blood pressure increases, and (b) two predisposing factors to chronic increases (hypertension). (p. 210–214)

7.   Describe two principal forms of coronary heart disease (CHD).   What limitation of traditional risk CHD factors led to a search for diatheses to CHD?   Describe Type A behavior as an early possibility and the confusion which resulted.   How may the idea of a Type D personality tie together this area?   Describe two possible biological diatheses. (p. 214–218)

Asthma (p. 218–221)

8.   What happens in an asthma attack?   Regarding the etiology of asthma, what question has been a topic of debate and what has research found?   Summarize research on psychological, family, and physiological predispositions to asthma. (p. 218–221)

AIDS: A Challenge for the Behavioral Sciences (p. 221–227)

9.   Why is AIDS an appropriate topic for an abnormal psychology textbook?   Briefly summarize the scope of the problem, description of the disease, and how it spreads. Describe efforts to prevent the spread of AIDS and their success.   Identify five reasons why knowledge about AIDS may not be sufficient to prevent its spread. (p. 221–227)

Gender and Health (p. 227–229)

10. Identify mortality and morbidity differences between men and women and possible biological and psychological explanations (one each). Summarize three other issues regarding gender and health. (p. 227–229)

Socioeconomic Status, Ethnicity, and Health (p. 229–231)

11. Illustrate the role of socioeconomic status and ethnicity on health in general. Identify five pathways or factors which may underlie these differences? (p. 229–231)

Therapies for Psychophysiological Disorders (p. 231–241)

12. Why are both medical and psychological interventions needed in treating psychophysiological disorders? Describe more specific programs in five areas: (a) hypertension (methods aimed at: risk factors, exercise, relaxation, and cognitions), (b) biofeedback, (c) Type A behavior, (d) stress management, and (e) pain management (acute and chronic). (p. 231–241)

Self-test, Chapter 8

(* Items not covered in Study Questions.)

Multiple-choice

*1. Which field specifically studies the role of psychological factors in health?
      a. Health psychology
      b. Psychiatry
      c. Clinical social work
      d. Pediatrics

2. Research using Holmes and Rahe's Social Readjustment Rating Scale found that
      a. agorophobics' symptoms were reduced when their spouses provided encouragement and support.
      b. a measure of social skills was related to criminals' recidivism rate.
      c. cognitive therapy led to improvements in learning disabled students' self-concept.
      d. health problems were related to the presence of stressful events in a person's life.

*3. Recent research findings on stress and illness indicate that there is a
      a. lack of association between stress and illness, contrary to researchers' hypotheses.
      b. correlation between stress and illness; the causal direction is not known.
      c. causal relationship between stress and illness; physical symptoms result in stressful life events.
      d. causal relationship between stress and illness; stressful life events cause physical symptoms.

4. William tends to react to stress by increased heart rate. Harold responds to stress with gastrointestinal distress. After a period of stress, William developed hypertension, and following the same stressful period, Harold developed an ulcer. What theory would explain this difference well?
      a. Conditioning theory
      b. Somatic-weakness theory
      c. Specific-reaction theory
      d. Multifactorial theory

*5. Systolic blood pressure is the amount of pressure when
      a. the heart is pumping.
      b. the heart is resting.
      c. the person is in motion.
      d. the person is in a relaxed position.

6. A recent research finding suggests that a risk factor for essential hypertension is
      a. the baseline level of blood pressure.
      b. cardiovascular reactivity.
      c. emotional temperament.
      d. time to return to normal blood pressure after stress.

7. The characteristic of Type A behavior that is best evaluated by structured interview is
      a. job involvement.
      b. fast pace of life.
      c. competitiveness.
      d. hostility.

8.   Simon experiences severe levels of anger, anxiety, and depression. His mood fluctuates closely with his job success, although he places a great deal of pressure upon himself to succeed. Simon would have Type D personality if
    a. he avoids expressing his emotional disposition.
    b. he freely discloses when he feels negative emotion.
    c. he also has coronary heart disease.
    d. he states that he dislikes his job.

9.   A central assumption in efforts to prevent AIDS is
    a. that individuals are rational in receiving prevention information.
    b. that the target group can process the information accurately.
    c. individuals at risk are interested in decreasing risk.
    d. more individuals seek opportunities to reduce risk when it is presented as an option.

10.   Relaxation training for hypertension is sometimes made more specific by
    a. focusing upon lowering sympathetic nervous system arousal.
    b. focusing upon lowering parasympathetic nervous system arousal.
    c. focusing upon specific muscle groups.
    d. None of the above choices are correct.

Short Answer

1.   Psychophysiological disorders are not a category in DSM-IV-TR because . . .

2.   Why was it difficult to apply Selye's theory of stress to psychology?

3.   Define "functional social support".

4.   Summarize the cognitive-behavioral approach to understanding stress-illness relationships.

5.   How does psychoanalysis account for the fact that people develop different psychophysiological disorders when exposed to the (apparently) same stressors?

6.   How important is essential hypertension as a health problem?

7.   What do people experience when they have an asthma attack?

8. Summarize one biological and one psychological explanation for the longer longevity of women.

9. List five pathways or factors which underlie health differences among various socioeconomic and ethnic groups.

10. Describe the treatment for Type A behavior.

Answers to Self-test, Chapter 8

Multiple-choice

1. a (p. 199)   2. d (p. 201)   3. d (p. 205)   4. c (p. 207)
5. a (p. 210)   6. d (p. 213)   7. d (p. 215–216)   8. a (p. 217)
9. a (p. 226)   10. a (p. 235)

Short Answer

1.   Virtually all physical diseases are recognized as potentially related to psychological stress. (p. 198)

2.   It was not clear how stress should be defined: in terms of stimuli, responses, or individual differences in ability to cope. (p. 200)

3.   The *quality* of an individual's friendships: having close friends that can be called on in time of need. (p. 204)

4.   While physical stresses are escapable, people may also have negative emotions and ineffective cognitive orientations that are not escapable and, thus, may be even more important in illness. (p. 209–2100

5.   Unconscious, unresolved conflicts influence how individuals respond to stress thus producing different disorders. (p. 209)

6.   Called the "silent killer" (because people aren't aware of and don't check their blood pressure), essential hypertension is the cause of 90% of cases of high blood pressure which contributes to many medical problems. (p. 210)

7.   Sudden onset with tightness in chest, wheezing, coughing. Increased fluid in lungs, eyes, etc. Fear of suffocation. (p. 219)

8.   Biologically women may be more protected; perhaps by estrogen. Psychologically women may less commonly exhibit Type A characteristics. (Both explanations are debated.) (p. 227–228)

9.   Social environment that does not emphasize healthy lifestyles. Increased stressors generally. Discrimination and prejudice. Limited access to health care. Acceptance of death as inevitable. (p. 229–231)

10.   Multifaceted programs encourage more relaxed behaviors (talk slower, listen more), reduce anger and stress from TV and work, cognitive changes to stop seeing everything as a challenge that must be met, reduce negative beliefs and emotions (p. 236)

9 Eating Disorders

Overview

This is the last of four chapters covering topics related to anxiety and stress. The previous chapters include Chapters 6 and 7 discussing psychological disorders related to anxiety and stress in various ways. Then Chapter 8 discusses the effects of anxiety and stress on medical illnesses and on the body generally. We have long recognized stress's contribution to the psychophysiological disorders (such as ulcers); however, that term has been dropped with recognition that stress can play a role in virtually all physical problems.

Chapter 9 turns to another set of disorders, eating disorders, which also involve physical effects of anxiety and stress. Eating disorders, such as anorexia nervosa, involve physical changes severe enough to be fatal. They certainly involve anxiety and stress. However, in this case, the anxiety and stress seem to result from cultural pressures on people, especially young women, to control their weight.

After Chapter 9, the text shifts to two disorders that are more complex: mood disorders such as depression (Chapter 10), and schizophrenia (Chapter 11). Both have been widely studied and, for various reasons, much of the research has focused on genetic and physiological issues.

Chapter Summary

Clinical Description of three disorders is provided. Anorexia nervosa involves inadequate food intake so that the victim, usually female, may starve to death. Bulimia, in which individuals gorge themselves then purge the food by vomiting or using laxatives, is not as life-threatening but can also have serious physical consequences. Binge eating disorder (a proposed diagnosis for further study) describes individuals who experience recurrent eating binges without purging or weight loss (indeed, commonly with weight gain or fluctuation). Binge eating disorder is not well understood and is not discussed further.

The *Etiology of Eating Disorders* appears to be complex and variable. Biological factors have been hypothesized based on genetic data and knowledge of brain mechanisms in eating. Sociocultural factors are strongly suggested by correlations between eating disorders and social pressure to be thin as reflected in advertising, etc. Other views have focused on personality, family, and abuse issues. Cognitive-behavioral views reformulate many of these ideas with emphasis on irrational beliefs about the necessity of being thin and about controlling eating in order to be socially acceptable.

The *Treatment of Eating Disorders* describes problems in treating these complex conditions. Biological treatment using antidepressants has yielded mixed results. In the short run anorexics can be kept alive by hospitalizing them to maintain their weight. Treatment of the issues underlying anorexia and bulimia has been more difficult. Family and cognitive-behavioral methods are used to address the potential combination of family, social, and psychological factors.

Essential Concepts

1.   Two long-recognized eating disorders are anorexia nervosa (in which people do not eat) and bulimia nervosa (in which people have eating binges followed by purging).

2.   Binge eating disorder, describes individuals who have eating binges without purging. It is proposed in DSM-IV-TR as a new diagnosis for further study.

3.   Eating disorders may have a genetic liability although adoption studies are needed. Brain chemicals involved in controlling normal appetite may be disrupted in individuals with an eating disorder although it is unclear whether this is a cause or a result of the eating disorder.

4.   Social pressures especially on women to be thin, to diet, etc. appear to be significant factors leading to eating disorders.

5.   Dynamic views stress developmental conflicts so that extreme thinness becomes a way to establish independence.

6.   Research points to personality, family, and child abuse characteristics. However some research is retrospective and difficult to interpret.

7.   Cognitive-behavioral views support other research and suggest these individuals have unrealistic beliefs about the necessity of being thin and/or have poor skills in moderating their eating. Personal beliefs and social pressures reinforce starvation. binging, etc.

8.   Antidepressants have shown some success in treating bulimia although dropout rates are high.

9.   Anorexics may require hospitalization to prevent starvation and manage medical complications.

10.   Treatment focuses on family therapy and on cognitive-behavioral methods to reinforce eating and challenge beliefs about being thin. Treatment of these underlying issues (and long-term weight maintenance) is difficult.

Key Terms

Anorexia nervosa (p. 246)

Bulimia nervosa (p. 248)

Binge eating disorder (p. 250)

Study Questions

Clinical Description (p. 246–251)

1. Three diagnostic labels are described. For each label summarize the (a) distinguishing features, (b) subtypes, (c) relationship to other psychological problems, (d) physical effects, and (e) prognosis. (Note that binge eating disorder is a tentative label and not yet well understood.) (p. 246–251)

Etiology of Eating Disorders (p. 251–261)

2. Under biological factors, what data suggest a genetic contribution to eating disorders? Identify three hypothesized physiological variables in eating disorders and research results. (p. 251–253)

3. Briefly describe social factors in eating disorders in four areas (sociocultural influences, gender influences, cross-cultural studies, and ethnic differences). (p. 253–256)

4.   Summarize the basis of eating disorders according to Bruch's psychodynamic view. Identify several personality, family, and child abuse factors in eating disorders and the quality of the research in each area. (p. 256–259)

5.   Summarize cognitive-behavioral views on anorexia nervosa and of bulimia nervosa. What factors are confirmed in the "tasting" research of Polivy and others.(p. 260–261)

Treatment of Eating Disorders (p. 261–266)

6.   Summarize the effectiveness of biological treatment of bulimia (including two problems) and of anorexia. (p. 262)

7.   Describe the goals, methods, and effectiveness of two stages in treating anorexia. Describe Minuchin's family therapy approach to the second stage. (p. 262–263)

8.   Describe a cognitive-behavioral approach to treatment of bulimia. Include description of both behavioral methods (to alter actual eating) and cognitive methods (to alter beliefs). (p. 263–264)

9.   Describe the outcomes of cognitive-behavioral treatments for bulimia including effects on other problems, comparisons with biological and interpersonal therapies, and remaining problems. (p. 264–266)

Self-test, Chapter 9

(* Items not covered in Study Questions.)

Multiple-choice

1.   A physiological effect of anorexia nervosa is
       a. hirsutism (growing heavier, darker hair).
       b. amenorrhea (loss or irregularity of menstrual period).
       c. high blood pressure.
       d. All of the above.

2.   The easiest way to distinguish between bulimia and anorexia nervosa is
       a. bingeing.
       b. a higher rate of psychological distress.
       c. pronounced weight loss.
       d. depression.

3.   The neurotransmitter most closely associated with eating disorders is
       a. epinephrine.
       b. dopamine.
       c. opioid.
       d. serotonin.

4.   Lydia is a white, upper-class woman with anorexia. Which of the following is most likely
       to also be true of Lydia?
       a. She has dieted before.
       b. She also has bulimia.
       c. She also has bipolar disorder.
       d. She reads many women's magazines.

* 5.   Studies of genetic influences on eating are most convincing for which problem?
       a. Anorexia nervosa
       b. Bulimia nervosa
       c. Obesity
       d. Binge eating disorder

6.   After looking through a fashion magazine, Daisy feels fat and is ashamed of her body. She
       doubts that she will ever be as thin as the models she sees in the magazine. Which theory
       explains Daisy's reactions to the magazine?
       a. Biosocial theory
       b. Expectancy theory
       c. Self-objectification theory
       d. Self-deprecating theory

7.   Studies of the personality of anorexics indicate that they are generally
       a. impulsive, adventurous, outgoing.
       b. confused, disoriented, withdrawn.
       c. shy, obedient, perfectionistic.
       d. warm, sensitive, helpful.

8. The first step in treating anorexia nervosa is
    a. medication to reduce anxiety about eating.
    b. education on the importance of a well balanced diet.
    c. hospitalization to promote and monitor eating.
    d. assessment to identify causes and plan individualized treatment.

9. The ultimate goal of Minuchin's family therapy in treating anorexia is to
    a. get the parents to take responsibility for their role in the problem.
    b. redefine the disorder as an interpersonal issue.
    c. force the patient to eat.
    d. quit trying to force their daughter to eat.

10. All of the following have been found to lessen the symptoms of bulimia *except*
    a. antidepressant medication.
    b. interpersonal psychotherapy.
    c. letting the bulimic binge but not allowing her to purge.
    d. the passage of time.

Short Answer

1. What are some physical side effects of the purging type of bulimia nervosa?

2. What data lead us to believe there a genetic diathesis for eating disorders?

3. How do cross-cultural data indicate the role of social/cultural factors in eating disorders?

4. Summarize Bruch's psychodynamic view of eating disorders.

5. What has research shown about the families of individuals with eating disorders?

6. How is the cognitive-behavioral view of bulimia different from its view of anorexia?

7. Describe what is done in "tasting" research studies by Polivy and others.

8. Describe the effectiveness of biological treatments for eating disorders.

9.   Describe cognitive methods to alter the beliefs of bulimic individuals.

10.   What problems remain in treating eating disorders?

Answers to Self-test, Chapter 9

Multiple-choice

1. b (p. 246)   2. c (p. 248)   3. d (p. 252)   4. a (p. 253)
5. c (p. 254)   6. c (p. 255)   7. c (p. 257–258)   8. c (p. 262)
9. b (p. 263)   10. d (p. 264–265)

Short Answer

1.   Menstrual irregularity. Frequent purging can change electrolyte balances, produce tooth decay from stomach acid, tissue damage, salivary glands can become swollen, etc. (p. 250)

2.   Eating disorders are much more likely in close relatives. Higher concordance in MZ than DZ twins. Linkage analysis results. These suggest a genetic diathesis — although adoptee studies have not been done. (p. 251)

3.   Eating disorders (and social emphasis on thinness) appear more prevalent in industrialized countries, although evidence is limited. (p. 255–256)

4.   Children are raised to feel ineffectual by parents who impose wishes on child while ignoring child's desires. Child does not learn to recognize internal needs (like hunger) and seizes on societal emphasis on thinness as way to be in control and have an identity. (p. 257)

5.   Variable studies. Disturbed relations and low support but may be result of eating disorder or problems in general. Limited results based on reports, not direct observations. (p. 258–259)

6.   Bulimics are assumed to be similar to anorexics except they have rigid self-rules about eating leading which are, inevitably, broken in binges. After binges, purging reduces their anxiety but lowers self-esteem so the cycle repeats. (p. 260)

7.   Participants drink a high-calorie milk shake (a "preload") then rate ice creams. Afterward they may eat the ice cream. People high in restrained dieting eat more ice cream. (p. 260–261)

8.   Anti-depressants are effective with bulimics although many drop out and effects last only as long as drug is taken. Drugs have not been effective in anorexia. (p. 262)

9.   Urged to identify, question, and change beliefs that weight is vital to acceptance by self and others, that only extreme dieting can control weight. (p. 264)

10.   Half the time patients do not respond to treatment, possibly because they also have other social or personal problems. (p. 265–266)

10 Mood Disorders

Overview

The previous four chapters covered a wide range of problems related, in one way or another, to anxiety and stress. They included both psychological disorders and medical conditions in which anxiety and stress are prominent.

The text now discusses two groups of disorders in which physiological factors have been widely studied. They are mood disorders such as depression and schizophrenia. Complex, and similar, physiological theories, especially involving neurotransmitters have been developed for these disorders. They are often described as involving brain imbalances.

Chapter 10 covers mood disorders, including lowered mood (depression) and heightened mood (mania). Chapter 10 also discusses suicide, which is often associated with depression. The literature on mood disorders is complex. Physiological and genetic factors have long been studied, both because drugs are effective in treating them and because manic individuals experience rapid mood shifts that often seemed otherwise inexplicable. Psychological research has also been extensive and psychological therapies have proven effective.

For similar reasons, physiological and genetic factors have long been suspected in schizophrenia (Chapter 11). Schizophrenia has been the subject of extensive research but remains a difficult problem to understand and to treat. Drugs are a core part of treatment but are only partially effective.

After Chapters 10 and 11, the text shifts to disorders in which social and behavioral issues seem more prominent.

Chapter Summary

The chapter begins by describing *General Characteristics of Mood Disorders*. DSM labels are based on the pattern and severity of depressive and manic episodes. Individuals with very different or heterogeneous behaviors receive the same label, suggesting other distinctions may be important.

Psychological Theories of Mood Disorders are well developed and varied. Psychoanalytic theory suggests that dependent people remain stuck in sadness because they cannot work through the anger that all people experience following a loss. Beck's cognitive theory suggests that depressives understand events through cognitive distortions that lead them to blame themselves for negative outcomes. Helplessness/hopelessness theory suggests that difficulty controlling negative events leads people to attribute the difficulty to themselves and feel hopeless about influencing outcomes — resulting in depression. An interpersonal approach suggests depressed individuals have fewer social supports, perhaps because their ineffective behaviors lead others to avoid them. Theories of mania are less well developed but view mania as a defense against depressing ideas about self.

Biological Theories of Mood Disorders are important because of a genetic predisposition, especially for bipolar disorders. Research indicates that depressives and manics have difficulty with certain brain neurotransmitters; however, the nature of this difficulty is unclear. Neuroendocrine difficulties are also suggested. Many believe these theories are all different aspects of, or ways of viewing, mood disorders and that an integrated approach is necessary.

Therapies for Mood Disorders include psychotherapeutic approaches derived from psychological theories of depression as well as somatic treatments including electroconvulsive shock and drugs. Considerable research has studied the relative effectiveness and utility of these approaches.

Depression in Childhood and Adolescence is relatively (but not totally) similar to adult depression. Treatment is largely psychological and based on the special needs of children.

Suicide is partially related to depression although many suicidal individuals are not obviously depressed. The text reviews basic facts and theories, describes approaches to preventing suicide, and discusses ethical issues in dealing with suicide.

Essential Concepts

NB

1. DSM-IV-TR lists two major mood disorders (major depression and bipolar disorder) and two chronic mood disorders (dysthymic and cyclothymic disorder).

2. Freud proposed that orally fixated people who experience a loss are unable to accept the anger that results so that they do not stop grieving and become depressed.

3. Beck suggests that depression results from cognitive schemata involving negative views of the self, the world, and the future.

4. The learned helplessness theory of depression evolved out of research that found depressive-like behaviors in animals exposed to inescapable aversive events. The current version emphasizes feelings of hopelessness that result from self-blame for aversive events.

5. Interpersonal approaches note that depressed people have fewer social supports, perhaps because their behaviors lead others to avoid them.

6. Mania (in bipolar disorder) is seen as a defense against depression, low self-esteem, or similar states.

7. Genetic data indicate a heritable component to major mood disorders, especially bipolar disorder.

8. Biological theories developed out of drug research and suggest problems with certain neurotransmitters or with hormones secreted in the brain.

9. Physiological and psychological theories of depression are probably two different ways to describe the same phenomenon.

10. Several psychological approaches, especially Beck's cognitive therapy, are widely used in treating depression.

11. A major NIMH study indicates that psychological treatment of depression is at least comparable to biological treatment in effectiveness.

12. There are a number of biological treatments for depression including electroconvulsive therapy and antidepressant drugs. Lithium is a useful drug in treating bipolar disorder. Some approaches can have serious side effects.

13. Depressed children are similar to depressed adults (but more suicide, guilt, etc.). Psychological treatments are effective.

14. While all people who commit suicide are not depressed, many people who are depressed think about or attempt taking their own life.

15. Specialized methods and suicide prevention centers have been developed to help people who are considering suicide.

16. Traditionally therapists have devoted themselves to preventing suicide although this can raise quality-of-life issues. More recent debates over physician-assisted suicide raise additional issues.

To My Students

This chapter covers both depression and the related topic of suicide. Estimates are that 20 percent of students will consider suicide during college. You might consider what you would do if a friend (or you) feels suicidal. You will find some ideas in the chapter. However, you would also want to seek professional help. Most areas of the United States have 24-hour telephone lines to suicide prevention centers as described on pages 312–313. This would be a good number to add to your address book. You can probably get the number from your instructor, college counseling center, or the local mental health clinic. Sometimes this is "911" but some 911 centers will refer you to another number.

Key Terms

Mood disorders (p. 268)

Depression (p. 268)

Mania (p. 268)

Major [or unipolar] depression (p. 269)

Bipolar I disorder (p. 270)

Mixed episode (p. 271)

Hypomania (p. 271)

Cyclothymic disorder (p. 271)

Dysthymic disorder (p. 272)

Logotherapy (p. 274)

Negative triad (p. 275)

Learned helplessness theory (p. 277)

Attribution (p. 278)

Tricyclic drugs (p. 284)   Anti.

Monoamine oxidase [MAO] inhibitors (p. 284)

Electroconvulsive therapy [ECT] (p. 297)

Bilateral ECT (p. 297)

Unilateral ECT (p. 297)

Lithium carbonate (p. 299)

Egoistic suicide (p. 308)

Altruistic suicide (p. 308)

Anomic suicide (p. 308)

Suicide prevention centers (p. 312)

Study Questions

General Characteristics of Mood Disorders (p. 268–273)

1. Give at least five different general characteristics of depression and of mania. Distinguish among the two major mood disorders (p. 269–270) and the two chronic mood disorders (p. 271–272) in DSM-IV-TR. What is meant by heterogeneity within the categories? (p. 270–271)

Psychological Theories of Mood Disorders (p. 273–283)

2. According to psychoanalytic theory what childhood circumstances predispose people to depression. How does (normal) bereavement develop into depression?. What is the current status of this theory? (p. 273–275)

3. Describe the three levels of cognitive activity that lead to depressed feelings according to Beck. Evaluate this theory by describing research on two points. (p. 275–277)

Dev V

4.   Describe three stages in the evolution of the helplessness/hopelessness theory of depression. What four problems remain? (p. 277–281)

5.   Summarize an interpersonal theory of depression by describing five interpersonal characteristics of depressed individuals. According to research, do these characteristics appear to precede or result from depression? (p. 281–282)

6.   Identify three psychological variables important in bipolar disorder? Describe a study suggesting that mania is a defense against low self-esteem. (p. 282–283)

Biological Theories of Mood Disorders (p. 283–287)

7.   What three research areas (starting on pages 283, 284, and 286) suggest biological factors in mood disorders?   What has genetic research found regarding inheritance of bipolar depression?   of unipolar depression? (p. 283–284)

8.   What are the theorized roles of norepinephrine and serotonin in mania and in depression? Describe the drug actions that led to these theories. Describe two research approaches used to evaluate these theories (and the limitation of each).   (p. 284–285)

9.   Which part of the neuroendocrine system has been linked to depression and how?   What do the neurotransmitter and neuroendocrine findings suggest about psychological theories of depression? Illustrate this point using an integrated theory of bipolar disorder. (p. 286–287)

Therapies for Mood Disorders (p. 287–300)

10.   Regarding psychological therapies for depression, briefly describe two psychodynamic therapies, and Beck's cognitive/behavior therapy. Describe a NIMH research program on treating depression including its importance, the groups and procedures, seven findings, and two controversies. Briefly describe three more recent therapies. (p. 287–296)

11.   Describe three approaches to psychological treatment of bipolar disorder. Describe three biological therapies including effectiveness, advantages, and disadvantages. (p. 296–300)

Depression in Childhood and Adolescence (p. 300–303)

12.   Compare child and adolescent depression to adult depression in regard to (a) symptoms, (b) prevalence, (c) etiology, and (d) biological and psychological therapies. (p. 300–303)

Suicide (p. 304–316)

13.   Review and be able to recognize 18 facts about suicide. As a general perspective on suicide summarize six research findings and four theories. (p. 304–310)

14.   According to psychological tests, what are three characteristics of people likely to, or not likely to, commit suicide? List two reasons it is difficult to use tests to predict who will commit suicide. (p.310–311)

15.   Summarize Schneidman's approach to suicide prevention and the general approach of suicide prevention centers. Identify two clinical and ethical issues health professionals face in preventing suicide. Under physician-assisted suicide describe Jack Kevorkian's early work, Oregon's law and it's aftermaths. (p. 311–313)

Self-test, Chapter 10

(* Items not covered in Study Questions.)

Multiple-choice

1. Jose has been depressed on and off for the past several years. When he is not depressed, however, he frequently feel elated and has high levels of energy. After these phases of alternating depressed and elevated mood, he experiences normal mood. Based on this information, which diagnosis best fits Jose during one of these cycles?
    a. Bipolar disorder
    b. Cyclothymic disorder
    c. Unipolar disorder
    d. Schizoaffective disorder

2. In Freud's theory of depression, _____ is the diathesis and _____ is the stress which together lead to depression.
    a. introjection; loss
    b. loss; introjection
    c. fixation at the oral stage; loss
    d. the Oedipal Complex; repression

3. James plays violin in the local symphony. A recent concert was poorly reviewed in a newspaper article, and James feels worthless and despondent. According to Beck, this is an example of which of the following cognitive distortions?
    a. selective abstraction
    b. overgeneralization
    c. arbitrary inference
    d. magnification

4. Which of the following is suggested by an interpersonal theory of depression?
    a. Depressive behaviors are reinforced by others seeking to cheer up the individual.
    b. Interpersonal trauma leads to withdrawal and depression.
    c. Depressed people withdraw from social contact and, over time, lose social skills.
    d. Poor social skills both lead to and result from depression.

5. Biological studies of the effects of antidepressant medications on neural chemistry rely upon
    a. measuring the neurotransmitter levels directly.
    b. principally brain-imaging techniques.
    c. measuring metabolites associated with the neurotransmitter.
    d. assessing the behavioral effects when the drug has been discontinued.

6. How effective is Beck's cognitive therapy for depression?
    a. more effective than psychoanalysis but less effective than drugs
    b. at least as effective as drugs
    c. effective only for mild forms of depression
    d. little research has been done on its effectiveness

7.   How does electroconvulsive therapy alleviate severe depression?
    a. It causes the patient to lose their memories of the events leading to the depression, enabling them to engage in therapy.
    b. The resulting epileptic seizure blocks the reuptake of serotonin.
    c. Neither a nor b; ECT is not an effective treatment for depression.
    d. Neither a nor b; it is not known by what mechanism ECT works.

8.   Which of the following symptoms are more common in children and adolescents with depression than in adults with depression?
    a. suicide attempts and guilt
    b. fatigue and suicidal ideation
    c. loss of appetite and early morning depression
    d. delusions

*9.   People who say they are going to kill themselves
    a. are at high risk for suicide.
    b. are only trying to get attention and won't actually commit suicide.
    c. are not usually depressed.
    d. will usually commit 'subintentioned' suicide.

10.   Suicide prevention centers focus upon
    a. the high degree of professional staff available for this line of work.
    b. the fact that many suicide attempts are accompanied by 'cries for help.'
    c. very public suicides, such as attempts to leap from buildings or bridges.
    d. none of the above choices are correct.

Short Answer

1.   List five characteristics of depression in addition to feeling sad.

2.   Summarize the latest version of the helplessness theory of depression.

3.   Describe a study suggesting that manic people try to conceal low self-esteem.

4.   What led to the development of norepinephrine theories of depression?

5.   How is the neuroendocrine system linked to depression?

6.   What do therapists do to treat depression based on cognitive theories of its cause?

7.   Identify one advantage and one disadvantage to drug treatment for serious depression.

8.   What is "subintended death" as a perspective on understanding suicide?

9.   Why has it been difficult to develop psychological tests to predict suicide?

10.   Describe Schneidman's approach to suicide prevention.

Answers to Self-test, Chapter 10

Multiple-choice

1. a (p. 271)   2. c (p. 274)   3. a (p. 275–276)   4. d (p. 281)
5. c (p. 284–285) 6. b (p. 288–289) 7. d (p. 297–298)   8. a (p. 300–301)
9. a (p. 306)   10. b (p. 311–312)

Short Answer

1. Change in sleep, eating, activity. Loss of interest, concentration, and energy. Social withdrawal. Negative feelings about self, thoughts of suicide. (p. 268)

2. Emphasizes hopelessness. Individuals have low self-esteem and attribute negative experiences to factors which are internal, stable, global. Thus they feel hopeless. (p. 279)

3. Maniac people reported good self-esteem but showed poor self-esteem on an indirect test (inferring esteem of the character in a short story). (p. 282–283)

4. Norepinephrine activity appeared to be the common factor underlying several groups of drugs that proved effective in treating depression. (p. 284

5. The neuroendocrine system consists of brain areas (hypothalamus, etc.) that release hormones which influence depression-related behaviors such as appetite, sleep. Overactivity in these areas could be part of depression. (p. 286)

6. Help clients identify and change their beliefs using logical analysis, providing contrary examples or experiences, etc. (p. 288–289)

7. Advantage: they hasten recovery. Disadvantages: drug side-effects, relapse common if drug is discontinued. May be prescribed by physicians with limited knowledge. (p. 298–299)

8. People may act in ways they know are ultimately self-destructive (for example; smoking) thus making it more difficult to understand and define suicide. (p. 307)

9. Tests cannot not predict situational factors. Also suicide is extremely infrequent so that no test can predict it accurately enough. (p. 311)

10. Schneidman emphasizes helping individuals find and consider other alternatives (also to reduce suffering, reconsider suicide). (p. 311–312)

11 Schizophrenia

Overview

Chapters 10 and 11 discuss two disorders that have been the subject of extensive research. Similar physiological theories have developed implicating brain neurotransmitters in both disorders. Mood disorders (Chapter 10) have been the subject of extensive psychological and physiological research with effective treatments emerging from both areas. Schizophrenia (Chapter 11) has led to even more extensive study, at least in part because no overt cure exists.

Of all the disorders covered in the text, schizophrenia comes closest to the common understanding of being "crazy". Despite extensive study, it remains a major concern both socially and scientifically. Historically, psychopathologists have disagreed on how to define schizophrenia and even on whether the term refers to one or to several different problems. Despite recent advances, no cure for schizophrenia has emerged. Currently a combination of approaches emphasizing drugs can manage, but not cure, the problem. Schizophrenics remain a major portion of mental hospital and health clinic patients.

After Chapter 11, the focus of the text shifts to disorders that often seem to be more social and behavioral in nature. These include substance abuse and dependence disorders (Chapter 12), personality disorders including antisocial personality disorder (Chapter 13), and sexual and gender identity disorders (Chapter 14). These problems do not easily fit traditional views of what constitutes a psychological disorder. Many involve behaviors that are more problematic for others than the individual. In many cases the individual does not appear disturbed in any obvious way aside from the problematic behavior itself. Such problems raise questions about how psychologists and society should view them.

Chapter Summary

Schizophrenia is a complex disorder and difficult to define. The *Clinical Symptoms of Schizophrenia* include positive symptoms (behavioral excesses or distortions), negative symptoms (behavioral deficits or lacks) and disorganized symptoms (overtly confused functioning).

The *History of the Concept of Schizophrenia* has included two traditions. Many American ideas about schizophrenia developed out of Bleuler's broad, psychoanalytically based definition. Recent DSM editions have moved toward Kraepelin's narrower, descriptive (rather than theoretical) approach, which has always been popular in Europe. Currently DSM-IV-TR recognizes three subtypes of schizophrenia. Disorganized schizophrenics exhibit blatantly bizarre and silly behaviors. Catatonic schizophrenics show primarily motor symptoms including wild excitement and apathetic withdrawal to the point of immobility. Paranoid schizophrenics have well-organized delusions of persecution, grandiosity, and jealousy. These subtypes have not been especially useful and current research seeks other useful ways to subcategorize schizophrenia.

Research on the *Etiology of Schizophrenia* has been extensive. Genetic, biochemical, and neurological data strongly suggest a biological diathesis to schizophrenia. Genetic data from family, twin, and more sophisticated adoptee studies all point to a genetic predisposition to schizophrenia. Biochemical research suggests excessive activity in nerve tracts of the brain that utilize the neurotransmitter dopamine. New neurological techniques suggest brain atrophy in schizophrenics with negative symptoms. Prenatal infections may be involved for these individuals.

Other research has looked at social class, family, and other variables. Schizophrenics are typically impoverished and research suggests their poverty is a result of their disability. Their families often have problems in communicating and handling conflict. These studies suggest stressors that may potentiate the diatheses suggested by biological research.

Many biological and psychological *Therapies for Schizophrenia* have been attempted. Antipsychotic drugs were a major advance in reducing the behavioral excesses of schizophrenia. However schizophrenics need additional help to cope with social living. Traditional psychotherapeutic approaches have not been effective, but recent social-skills, family, and behavioral methods show promise. There remains a need to integrate skills and knowledge of various disciplines in order to help schizophrenics lead as normal a life as possible.

Essential Concepts

1. Most symptoms of schizophrenia can be grouped into positive symptoms (or behavioral excesses such as confused thinking and speaking) and negative symptoms (or behavioral deficits including lack of energy, interest, and feelings).

2. Historic definitions of schizophrenia included Kraepelin's concept of dementia praecox and Bleuler's concept of loose associative threads. Currently DSM-IV-TR has moved to Kraepelin's narrower definition.

3. DSM-IV-TR defines three major subcategories of schizophrenia: disorganized, catatonic, and paranoid. These subcategories are limited. Research suggests the distinction between positive and negative symptoms may provide more useful distinctions.

4. Evidence from family, twin, and adoptee studies indicates a substantial genetic diathesis to schizophrenia, although this alone cannot fully explain the disorder's etiology.

5. Extensive research links dopamine activity in particular brain tracts to schizophrenia. The evidence suggests that both genetic and prenatal factors may lead to dopamine tract changes.

6. There is a link between low social status and schizophrenia. Sociogenic and social-selection explanations have been offered for this correlation.

7. Early theories that family issues cause schizophrenia have been discredited. However family patterns of communication and emotional expression may affect the post-hospital adjustment of schizophrenics.

8. Children of schizophrenic patients have been studied longitudinally in high-risk projects which shed light on the etiology of schizophrenia.

9.   Currently no treatments of schizophrenia are totally effective.   Neuroleptic medications are effective in controlling the positive symptoms of schizophrenia.

10.   Social skills, family, and cognitive-behavioral approaches show promise in improving the social adjustment of schizophrenics.

11.   There remains a need to integrate the skills of many disciplines to better help schizophrenics.

To My Students

Schizophrenia is a serious and complex problem.   Traditional paradigms have generated a tremendous amount of research.   Unfortunately no paradigm has proven highly useful and our understanding of this problem remains limited.

As a result this chapter spends little time describing paradigms and considerable time summarizing research.   At times the discussion becomes unavoidably complex, especially when summarizing the genetic and physiological research.   You may want to refer to the basic discussion of these topics in Chapter 2 of the text, especially pages 21 to 24.

The study questions indicate the core ideas to look for as you study.   Take your time and ask your instructor if you have questions.

Key Terms

Schizophrenia (p. 319)

Positive symptoms (p. 319)

Delusions (p. 320)

Hallucinations (p. 321)

Negative symptoms (p. 321)

Avolition (p. 321)

Alogia (p. 321)

Anhedonia (p. 322)

Flat affect (p. 322)

Asociality (p. 322)

Disorganized symptoms (p. 322)

Thought disorder (p. 322)

Disorganized speech (p. 322)

Incoherence (p. 323)

Loose associations (p. 323)

Derailment (p. 323)

Bizarre [behavior] (p. 323)

Catatonia (p. 323)

Catatonic immobility (p. 323)

Waxy flexibility (p. 324)

Inappropriate affect (p. 324)

Dementia praecox (p. 324)

Delusional disorder (p. 326)

Disorganized schizophrenia (p. 327)

Catatonic schizophrenia (p. 327)

Paranoid schizophrenia (p. 327)

Grandiose delusions (p. 327)

Delusional jealousy (p. 327)

Ideas of reference (p. 327)

Undifferentiated schizophrenia (p. 328)

Residual schizophrenia (p. 328)

Labeling theory (p. 329)

Dopamine theory (p. 333)

Sociogenic hypothesis (p. 338)

Social-selection theory (p. 338)

Schizophrenogenic mother (p. 338)

Expressed emotion [EE] (p. 339)

Prefrontal lobotomy (p. 344)

Antipsychotic drugs (p. 344)

Study Questions

Clinical Symptoms of Schizophrenia (p. 319–324)

1.   Summarize eleven symptoms of schizophrenia organized into four categories.   Give examples of the various terms explaining why they fit into the categories. (p. 319–324)

History of the Concept of Schizophrenia (p. 324–328)

2.   Describe Kraepelin's and Bleuler's early views on schizophrenia.   Trace the way Bleuler's view broadened in America.   List five ways in which the newer DSM definitions of schizophrenia have moved toward the narrower, European, view. (p. 324–326)

3.   Summarize several distinguishing characteristics of each of the three subtypes of schizophrenia in DSM-IV-TR.   Evaluate these subtypes by describing (a) their limitations and (b) another approach to subdividing schizophrenia. (p. 326–328)

Etiology of Schizophrenia (p. 328–341)

4. Describe and evaluate three approaches to studying genetic factors in schizophrenia. Summarize the overall importance of genetic factors and three limitations. (p. 328–332)

5. Why does genetic evidence suggest the need to study biochemical factors in schizophrenia? Summarize two reasons to believe dopamine activity is a factor in schizophrenia. Summarize current views on (a) dopamine levels vs. dopamine receptors and (b) positive vs. negative symptoms. How could different neural pathways allow prefrontal underactivity to effect both negative symptoms and, indirectly, positive symptoms? Identify four weaknesses to current dopamine theory. (p. 332–334)

6. Summarize data implicating (a) enlarged ventricles and (b) the prefrontal cortex in schizophrenia. Summarize data suggesting these differences may result from (a) birth complications or (b) viral infection before birth. (p. 335–337)

7.   What is the relationship between social class and schizophrenia? (What does it mean to say this is not a "continuous progression"?) Describe two theories of this relationship and two studies comparing the theories. (p. 337–338)

8.   Describe and evaluate four areas of possible family influence on schizophrenia. What did early developmental studies indicate about children who, later, became schizophrenic? What was the limitation of these studies and how did high-risk studies help? What have high-risk studies found (especially regarding positive and negative symptoms)? (p. 338–341)

Therapies for Schizophrenia (p. 341–355)

9.   Why were earlier biological treatments for schizophrenia abandoned? What are the benefits of and the problems with traditional antipsychotic drugs? What side effects are common? How have newer drug therapies helped? Evaluate the role of drugs in treating schizophrenia (p. 343–347)

10. The text describes three general psychological treatment approaches and three recent cognitive-behavioral approaches. For each, describe the (a) rationale, (b) method, and (c) results — if any. Summarize the origins and rationale of case management. (p. 347–352)

11. Summarize general trends in treatment in terms of the overall trend and four specific points. Identify four ongoing issues in the care of patients with schizophrenia. (p. 352–355)

Self-test, Chapter 11

(* Items not covered in Study Questions.)

Multiple-choice

* 1.   Schizophrenia is _____ researched and _____ understood.
    a. widely: well
    b. widely: poorly
    c. sparsely: well
    d. sparsely: poorly

2.   Which of the following are examples of negative symptoms of schizophrenia?
    a. Blunted emotions, lack of initiative.
    b. Hallucinations and delusions.
    c. Difficulty concentrating, low intelligence, poor memory.
    d. Catatonic immobility, waxy flexibility.

3.   Using the DSM-IV-TR, Janice is diagnosed as having Borderline Personality Disorder. Had she been diagnosed in 1950, she would have most likely been labeled with
    a. delusional disorder.
    b. bipolar disorder.
    c. schizophrenia.
    d. dementia praecox.

4.   Diagnoses of schizophrenia cannot be made if the patient also has
    a. anxiety.
    b. mood disorder.
    c. aggression.
    d. hypochondriasis.

5.   Which of the following findings presents a serious challenge to the theory of schizophrenia that proposes an excess amount of dopamine to be at the core of this disorder?
    a. Antipsychotic drugs relieve the symptoms of both drug psychoses and the psychosis of schizophrenia.
    b. Homovanillic acid, the major metabolite of dopamine, is not present in greater amounts in schizophrenics.
    c. Positive symptoms of schizophrenia are reduced by antipsychotic drugs more than negative symptoms.
    d. None of the above represent a challenge to the dopamine activity theory.

6.   In which parts of the brain of schizophrenics are abnormalities most commonly found?
    a. Temporal and parietal lobes.
    b. Limbic system and prefrontal cortex.
    c. Corpus collossum and amygdala.
    d. Diffuse lesions throughout the brain.

7. Mr. Bradley was diagnosed as schizophrenic seven years ago. Prior to the onset of his illness, he was attending medical school and planning to be a pediatrician. However, his bizarre symptoms such as delusions and hallucinations made it impossible for him to finish school, and after attempting a series of lower-level jobs, Mr. Bradley gave up on being able to keep a job or earn a living. He now lives in a run-down hotel on skid row. Mr. Bradley's story fits the _____ theory of social class and schizophrenia.
   a. schizophrenogenic
   b. high-risk
   c. sociogenic
   d. social-selection

8. Research investigating the role of the family in schizophrenia best supports the
   a. schizophrenogenic mother theory.
   b. triangulation theory.
   c. expressed emotion theory.
   d. labeling theory.

9. For what reason do patients with schizophrenia typically stop taking medication when they are discharged from the hospital?
   a. The side effects are unpleasant.
   b. Their psychiatrist determines that their illness is improved sufficiently so that they do not need to take daily medications.
   c. Their after-care programs emphasize psychological treatments and discourage reliance on medication, which is seen as a "crutch".
   d. They prefer their hallucinations to the monotony of daily existence.

10. This first person to use psychotherapy in treating people with schizophrenia was
   a. Sigmund Freud.
   b. Emil Kraepelin.
   c. Harry Stack Sullivan.
   d. Frieda Fromm-Reichmann.

Short Answer

1. What characteristics of the problem were emphasized by (a) Kraepelin's term "dementia praecox" and (b) Bleuler's term "schizophrenia"?

2. What diagnosis is appropriate for Russell? He believes he has the instant answer to all the country's problems. When people avoid him (because he constantly lectures them on the topic) he decides they fear the president will hear his ideas and instantly implement them. The president happened to be in town and Russell walked in assuming the president had come specifically to see him. When body guards threw him out, Russell became irate and declared the president was having sex with his wife and, thus, had refused to see him.

3. What has happened as a result of the low reliability of DSM-IV-TR subcategories of schizophrenia?

4.   Describe the data which most convincingly point to a genetic factor in the etiology of schizophrenia.

5.   Why does genetic data suggest the need to study biochemical factors in schizophrenia?

6.   Why is it significant that schizophrenics may have enlarged ventricles?

7.   Summarize data suggesting that viral complications contribute to neurological changes in schizophrenia.

8.   Explain what the text means in saying that the relation between schizophrenia and social class is not a continuous progression.

9.   What do "case managers" do in treating schizophrenia and why?

10.   Identify four ongoing issues in the care of patients with schizophrenia.

Answers to Self-test, Chapter 11

Multiple-choice

1. b (p. 319)   2. a (p. 321–322)   3. c (p. 325)   4. b (p. 326)
5. b (p. 333)   6. b (p. 335)   7. d (p. 338)   8. c (p. 340)
9. a (p. 344–345)   10. c (p. 347)

Short Answer

1. (a) early onset and progressive intellectual deterioration, (b) underlying difficulty in thinking and communication. (p. 324–325)

2. Paranoid schizophrenia. (p. 327)

3. There is much interest in finding better ways to subdivide schizophrenia, perhaps by distinguishing schizophrenics with positive, negative, and mixed symptoms. (p. 327–328)

4. Adoptee studies which indicate high rates of schizophrenia in children of schizophrenic mothers even though the children were raised by others. Earlier family and twin studies are not as convincing. (p. 331–332)

5. Because a genetic factor can only lead to schizophrenic behavior by influencing biochemical processes leading to the behavior. (p. 332)

6. If ventricles (natural openings in the brain) are enlarged, then the brain has shrunk with loss of brain cells or cell connections. (p. 335)

7. Schizophrenia was more common in people whose mothers were exposed to the influenza virus during their second trimester of pregnancy. (p. 336–337)

8. Schizophrenia is decidedly (not just relatively) more common in the lowest social classes. (p. 337)

9. They coordinate the services provided by a team and others in the community. Research shows that intensive, coordinated, community services reduce hospitalization costs and improve adjustment in many areas. (p. 352)

10. (1) providing aftercare after hospital release, (2) helping them obtain employment, (3) assisting them in living in the community, (4) preventing substance abuse. (p. 354–355)

12 Substance-Related Disorders

Overview

The previous two chapters covered mood disorders and schizophrenia. Similar, complex physiological theories have developed around each. Physiological research and theory for the remaining disorders in the text are not as extensive.

The next three chapters discuss disorders that have strong social and behavioral components. Chapter 12 discusses substance-related disorders including abuse of alcohol, nicotine, marijuana, and hard drugs. Chapter 13 covers personality disorders in which persistent and maladaptive personality traits or behaviors cause difficulty for the individual and others. The most well known personality disorder is the antisocial personality or psychopath characterized by antisocial behavior and/or by lack of guilt over that behavior. Chapter 14 will discuss a wide range of disorders involving sexual behavior.

Many of these problems involve behaviors that are maladaptive or socially unacceptable but not necessarily "disordered" in the traditional sense. Many are more bothersome to others than to the person involved. At times it can be difficult to decide if they are psychological, legal, or moral/ethical problems. This can present dilemmas for treatment personnel.

The text's coverage of specific problems will conclude with Chapters 15 and 16, which deal with issues and disorders of childhood and old age.

Chapter Summary

Drugs have always been used, and abused, to alter mood and consciousness. Contemporary practice distinguishes between substance abuse that affects daily functioning and substance dependence that also produces physiological changes leading to physical tolerance (or decreasing effects) and withdrawal reactions. The chapter discusses five groups of commonly abused substances.

Alcohol Abuse and Dependence produces short-term effects including poor judgment and coordination and long-term effects including addiction and physical deterioration. Alcoholism is a widespread social problem and much effort has gone into treating it. However results are limited and many alcoholics relapse.

Nicotine and Cigarette Smoking is still common despite strong evidence of health risks. *Marijuana* produces a "high" characterized by decreased cognitive and psychomotor functioning. Long-term use has physical and psychological effects. Debate continues over its possible uses in medical treatment.

Sedatives and Stimulants which, respectively, decrease and increase responsiveness, include several illegal and addictive drugs. Withdrawal is difficult (sometimes dangerous). *LSD and Other Hallucinogens* were originally studied, and are now abused, for their mind-altering properties.

Research into *The Etiology of Substance Abuse and Dependence* has identified many cultural, psychological, and biological variables. For example individual beliefs about the drug's effects and general personality variables influence alcohol's effects.

Therapy for Alcohol Abuse and Dependence describes a number of biological and psychological approaches. None are highly effective and a combination of programs tailored to each individual is needed. *Therapy for the Use of Illicit Drugs* begins with management of withdrawal problems followed by various biological and/or psychological approaches. All are of limited effectiveness. *Treatment of Cigarette Smoking* describes psychological and biological treatments that are moderately effective in smoking cessation, however, relapse is a major problem.

Prevention of Substance Abuse notes the social and pragmatic value of prevention programs, especially those directed at adolescents. Tobacco prevention programs, in particular, are common and effective methods are becoming apparent.

Essential Concepts

1.   Substance abuse involves use of a drug to the extent that it interferes with functioning. Substance dependence involves more serious interference plus withdrawal reactions and increased tolerance.

2.   Alcohol is an addicting drug that exacts a high cost from many individuals and from our society.

3.   Alcohol's short-term physiological effects are complex and mediated by cognitive expectancies. The long-term consequences can be quite severe both psychologically and biologically.

4.   Cigarette smoking is a tremendous health problem for smokers, for those near them, and for society at large.

5.   Marijuana interferes with cognitive functioning and psychomotor performance and appears to have some adverse physical effects with long-term use. However it also has therapeutic uses.

6.   Sedatives or "downers" reduce the body's responsiveness. They include organic narcotics and synthetic barbiturates.

7.   Sedatives are highly addictive and have important social consequences. For example, criminal behavior may result from an addict's attempt to maintain the expensive habit.

8.   Stimulants (amphetamines and cocaine) are "uppers" that heighten alertness and increase autonomic activity. They are also addictive.

9.   LSD and other hallucinogens produce a state that was once thought to mimic psychosis, and is characterized by sometimes dramatic changes in perception and cognition.

10. Sociocultural, psychological, and biological factors contribute to starting and continuing abuse.

11. Therapy for alcohol and drug abuse usually begins with detoxification. Various biological and psychological therapies are difficult to evaluate but only modestly effective.

12. Most ex-smokers quit spontaneously. Psychological and biological approaches are effective in the short run; however, relapse is an issue.

13. Prevention remains the most effective approach to controlling substance abuse. Effective prevention programs are growing, especially in preventing tobacco use among adolescents.

Key Terms

Substance dependence (p. 358)

Tolerance (p. 358)

Withdrawal (p. 358)

Substance abuse (p. 358)

Delirium tremens (DTs) (p. 359)

Polydrug abuse (p. 360)

Fetal alcohol syndrome (p. 364)

Nicotine (p. 365)

Secondhand smoke (p. 367)

Marijuana (p. 368)

Hashish (p. 368)

Sedatives (p. 372)

Opiates (p. 372)

Opium (p. 372)

Morphine (p. 372)

Heroin (p. 372)

Hydrocodone (p. 373

Oxycodone (p. 373)

Barbiturates (p. 374)

Stimulants (p. 375)

Amphetamines (p. 375)

Methamphetamine (p. 376)

Cocaine (p. 377)

LSD (p. 378)

Hallucinogen (p. 378)

Flashbacks (p. 379)

Mescaline (p. 379)

Psilocybin (p. 379)

MDMA (p. 379)

MDA (p. 379)

Ecstasy (p. 380)

Nitrous oxide (p. 381)

Detoxification (p. 389)

Antabuse (p. 390)

Covert sensitization (p. 393)

Controlled drinking (p. 394)

Heroin substitutes (p. 398)

Heroin antagonists (p. 398)

Methadone (p. 398)

Cross-dependent (p. 398)

Clonidine (p. 399)

Study Questions

1. Identify and distinguish between substance dependence and substance abuse in DSM-IV-TR. (p. 358–359)

Alcohol Abuse and Dependence (p. 359–365)

2.   What are the indicators of alcohol dependence and alcohol abuse? (p. 359–360) Describe the course of the disorder in Jellinek's analysis and current data on his analysis. Describe the short-term effects and long-term effects of alcohol abuse. (p. 359–365)

Nicotine and Cigarette Smoking (p. 365–368)

3.   How prevalent and serious is smoking? What are the consequences of secondhand smoke? (p. 365–368)

Marijuana (p. 368–372)

4.   Describe changes in prevalence of marijuana use. Summarize the psychological, somatic, and therapeutic effects of marijuana. (p. 369–372)

Sedatives and Stimulants (p. 372–378)

5. The text identifies two groups of sedatives and two groups of stimulants. For each group, describe (a) short-term effects, (b) long-term effects, and (c) withdrawal effects. (p. 372–378)

LSD and Other Hallucinogens (p. 378–382)

6. Summarize the history of LSD and other hallucinogens. What are the general effects of hallucinogens and what variables influence their effects? What is known about the short-term and long-term effects of ecstasy and PCP? (p. 378–382)

Etiology of Substance Abuse and Dependence (p. 382–388)

7.   Why is it difficult to make clear statements about the etiology of substance abuse and dependence? Identify five sociocultural variables affecting abuse and dependence (starting with cross-national variations). (p. 382–384)

8.   The text describes three psychological variables in substance abuse. For mood alteration, describe the relationship between tension-reduction and (a) cognition and perception (b) consumption and stress and (c) expectations. Describe the role of beliefs about risks and prevalence. For personality and drug use, describe the role of negative affect and desire for arousal/novelty. What may be a biological diathesis for alcoholism? (p. 384–388)

Therapy for Alcohol Abuse and Dependence (p. 388–397)

9.   Why is admitting the problem often an issue with alcoholics? Describe and evaluate traditional hospital treatment of alcoholism. How are biological treatments best viewed? Identify three ways in which drugs may be helpful. Describe and evaluate five treatments for alcoholism (including three variations on cognitive/behavioral methods). Identify four, more general, clinical considerations in treating alcoholics. (p. 388–397)

Therapy for the Use of Illicit Drugs (p. 397–400)

10. What is the central or first step in treating drug addiction? Describe and evaluate two biological and four psychological approaches to treatment of drug abuse. (p. 397–400)

Treatment of Cigarette Smoking (p. 401–404)

11. In treating smoking, how effective and common are self-help programs. Briefly identify six psychological approaches to treating smoking. Identify four biological treatments for smoking and discuss their effectiveness. Identify a number of approaches to relapse prevention? (p. 401–404)

Prevention of Substance Abuse (p. 404–406)

12. Why are prevention programs important? (p. 404–405) Describe seven common components of tobacco prevention programs (and note which ones are counterproductive). (p. 405–406)

Self-test, Chapter 12

(* Items not covered in Study Questions.)

Multiple-choice

1. Wanda drinks frequently, and now does not require as much alcohol as six months ago to achieve the same effect. She reports that she can out drink most people. Wanda is probably
    a. genetically not predisposed to alcoholism.
    b. developing a physiological dependence on alcohol.
    c. acquiring behavioral skills in modulating her drinking.
    d. deluding herself. This is not physically possible.

*2. Cigarette smoking is more prevalent among
    a. women.
    b. the elderly.
    c. college students.
    d. blue-collar workers.

*3. Which of the following statements about the "stepping-stone" theory of drug use is most accurate?
    a. Most people who use "soft" drugs will move on to try "harder" drugs.
    b. Most people who use "hard" drugs started out on "softer" drugs.
    c. There is no difference between "hard" and "soft" drugs.
    d. There is no relationships between the use of "hard" and "soft" drugs.

4. Jolynn took a drug that caused the following symptoms: she felt wide awake and friendly, and had no interest in lunch despite not having eaten since the night before. After taking a second dose of the drug, she became nervous and confused, and developed a severe headache. Which of the following drugs did Jolynn probably take?
    a. alcohol
    b. marijuana
    c. a barbiturate
    d. an amphetamine

5. Which drug produces euphoria, drowsiness, reverie, and sometimes a lack of coordination?
    a. cocaine
    b. heroin
    c. LSD
    d. amphetamines

6. An important sociocultural variable that has been cited in the increased use of cigarettes has been
    a. the role of the family in providing implicit messages regarding smoking.
    b. rebound effects from the end of 'just say no' campaigns.
    c. the media and advertising.
    d. the restriction of places where one may smoke.

7. Marsha's mother is an alcohol abuser, and she is concerned with determining whether her own drinking patterns put her at risk for similar problems. Which of the following considerations would assist her in determining if her drinking is a problem?
    a. Making rules for herself about when to drink.
    b. Eagerly awaiting her first drink after work.
    c. Annoyance when her husband talks to her about her drinking habits.
    d. All of the above are signs of alcohol abuse.

8. When treating an alcoholic, it is important to
    a. consider the role that drinking plays in the person's life.
    b. determine the biological basis for the person's drinking problem.
    c. adhere closely to a particular theoretical model to avoid confusing the patient with contradictory approaches.
    d. focus on treating the drinking problem first, before trying to tackle other life problems which the person may be experiencing.

9. Which of the following drugs is most likely to have life-threatening withdrawal reactions?
    a. alcohol
    b. barbiturates
    c. heroin
    d. cocaine

10. Which has been the most difficult problem among smokers trying to quit?
    a. Making the decision to quit.
    b. Obtaining professional help.
    c. Preventing relapse.
    d. Side-effects of cigarette substitutes.

Short Answer

1. What is the current status of Jellinek's theory of the course of alcoholism?

2. How serious is second hand smoke? Explain.

3. What has research shown about the therapeutic effects of marijuana?

4. What are the withdrawal effects of opium-based narcotics?

5. What events led to LSD being popularized in the 1960s?

6.   What is inherited as the genetic predisposition to alcoholism?

7.   Disulfiram or Antabuse can discourage alcoholics from drinking by (doing what).

8.   What happens in self-help programs for drug addiction?

9.   How effective are biological treatments for cigarette smoking?

10. What is the rationale of prevention programs?

Answers to Self-test, Chapter 12

Multiple-choice

1. b (p. 358)   2. d (p. 367)   3. b (p. 369)   4. d (p. 376)
5. b (p. 373)   6. c (p. 384)   7. d (p. 389)   8. a (p. 395)
9. b (p. 397)   10. c (p. 404)

Short Answer

1. Research indicates much more variability than his theory proposed. A few people progress from social drinking to skid row. More commonly, people fluctuate back and forth over time. (p. 361–3620

2. Quite serious. Kills 50,000 per year. Problems include lung damage, cardiovascular disease, birth complications, and respiratory infections. (p. 367–368)

3. Research confirms effective in reducing pain, nausea, and loss of appetite from cancer and cancer treatment. (p. 371)

4. Withdrawal effects resemble influenza and include sneezing, sweating, and (later) cramps, chills, sleeplessness. Diarrhea and vomiting may occur. (p. 374)

5. Harvard LSD researchers began using it themselves, leading to a scandal. They were dismissed from Harvard and founded an organization that publicized and popularized LSD. (p. 380)

6. Inherit the ability to tolerate and drink large quantities of alcohol. (p. 388)

7. Producing violent vomiting if one drinks alcohol after taking it. (p. 390)

8. Residential programs remove addicts from social pressures, support nonuse, provide charismatic role models, include confrontive group therapy, respect addicts as human beings. (p. 400)

9. Research indicates they are of some, but limited, help. They work best when combined with behavioral treatments for psychological factors. (p. 402–403)

10. Prevention, especially with adolescents, is much easier and more effective than treatment after the problem develops. (p. 404)

13 Personality Disorders

Overview

This is the second of three chapters on problems characterized by socially problematic behaviors or traits. Generally, these are not considered "mental illnesses" as the term is commonly used. However they do cause considerable unhappiness for affected individuals and/or for those around them.

Chapter 12 covered substance-related problems including alcohol and drug abuse and dependence. Chapter 13 discusses personality disorders in which people exhibit long-term patterns of thought and behavior that are ineffective, maladaptive, or socially unacceptable. Examples include social withdrawal, self-centeredness, and criminal activity. Chapter 14 will deal with problematic sexual behaviors. These include sexual disorders or deviations, such as fetishism and rape, as well as sexual dysfunctions or inadequacies such as impotence.

Many of the problems in these chapters are characterized by socially disapproved behaviors. Often others want the person to change more than the person does. This raises difficult issues: can (or should) psychologists change people who do not especially seek change? Are psychologists acting as helpers, as law enforcers, or as moral authorities? Such issues are difficult to answer.

After Chapter 14, the next two chapters cover disorders and issues of childhood (Chapter 15) and old age (Chapter 16). They will complete the text's discussion of psychological disorders. In Chapters 17 and 18 the text will turn to general issues in abnormal psychology.

Chapter Summary

Personality disorders are long-standing, pervasive, inflexible patterns that impair the individual's functioning in society. *Classifying Personality Disorders; Clusters, Categories, and Problems* presents basic issues in categorizing and applying these labels reliably.

In DSM, personality disorders are organized into three clusters. The *Odd/Eccentric Cluster* consists of the paranoid, schizoid, and schizotypal personality disorders. All three have characteristics that seem related to schizophrenia although research evidence is limited.

The *Dramatic/Erratic Cluster* consists of borderline, histrionic, narcissistic, and antisocial personality disorders. Various theories suggest that all result from forms of distorted and limited parent/child relationships. Antisocial personality disorder is similar to the concept of psychopathy. Research suggests that psychopaths come from families that provided little discipline, love, or effective role models. They experience limited anxiety or empathy in research studies.

The *Anxious/Fearful Cluster* consists of avoidant, dependent, and obsessive-compulsive personality disorders. Their causes are not widely studied (perhaps because such people are less overtly problematic or obvious to others).

Therapies for Personality Disorders typically must focus on an acute problem which brought the person to therapy as well as the underlying personality disorder. Borderline personalities present major challenges and a number of therapists have adapted therapy approaches for them. Psychological and somatic treatment of psychopaths has been considered hopeless traditionally. Prisons remain the common way of handling psychopaths but are effective only is isolating them from society — at least for awhile.

Essential Concepts

1.   Personality disorders are characterized by inflexible and pervasive traits that interfere with functioning. These Axis II diagnoses are problematic and dimensional classification may help.

2.   Ten personality disorders are defined in DSM-IV-TR organized into three clusters.

3.   Paranoid, schizoid, and schizotypal personality disorders (the odd/eccentric cluster) have unusual or withdrawn behaviors reminiscent of schizophrenia although research support is limited.

4.   Borderline, histrionic, narcissistic, and antisocial personality disorders comprise the dramatic/erratic cluster. Childhood problems have been suspected in these disorders.

5.   Antisocial personality disorder is related to psychopathy which has been widely studied.

6.   Research indicates that psychopaths come from families with antisocial role models, poor discipline, and little love. They experience little anxiety or empathy. In fact, they appear to suppress anxiety.

7.   Avoidant, dependent, and obsessive-compulsive personality disorders (the anxious/fearful cluster) are not well understood.

8.   Therapies for personality disorders are poorly worked out — probably because these people typically seek help for acute problems that arose out of the personality disorder.

9.   Borderline personalities present particular challenges for therapists. A number of therapists have developed particular therapy approaches for borderlines.

10. Efforts to change antisocial personality disorders have been unsuccessful. Psychotherapeutic and drug approaches have been of limited value as have prisons, the typical treatment method. Prisons do, however, isolate psychopaths until they become older and less of a threat to society.

Key Terms

Personality disorders (p. 409)

Paranoid personality (p. 411)

Schizoid personality (p. 412)

Schizotypal personality (p. 412)

Borderline personality (p. 413)

Histrionic personality (p. 416)

Narcissistic personality (p. 417)

Antisocial personality (p. 418)

Psychopathy (p. 418)

Avoidant personality (p. 424)

Dependent personality (p. 425)

Obsessive-compulsive personality (p. 425)

Dialectical behavior therapy (p. 429)

Study Questions

1. Define personality disorders as a group. How are they different from normal personality styles? (p. 409)

Classifying Personality Disorders: Clusters, Categories, and Problems (p. 410–411)

2.   Why are personality disorders placed on Axis II of DSM? Identify two problems in applying these diagnoses and explain how dimensional classification may help. (p. 410–411) Identify the three clusters of personality disorders (starting on pages 411, 413, and 424).

Odd/Eccentric Cluster (p. 411–413)

3.   Identify and briefly describe the three disorders in the odd/eccentric cluster. Be able to distinguish them from each other and from similar Axis I disorders. What idea has guided the search for causes of these disorders and how well has this idea proven out so far? (p. 411–413)

Dramatic/Erratic Cluster (p. 413–424)

4.   For borderline personality disorder, describe the disorder and three views on its etiology. For the next two disorders, describe the disorder and summarize a psychoanalytic view of its etiology. (p. 413–418)

5. Define (and distinguish between) the terms "antisocial personality disorder" and "psychopathy". Summarize data on the role of the family and on genetic factors in psychopathy. Why is it desirable to have data on the role of the family that is not retrospective? (p. 418–422)

6. Regarding emotion and psychopathy, summarize research in three areas indicating little anxiety and one area indicating little empathy in psychopaths. Also summarize research on response modulation indicating that psychopaths respond impulsively. (p. 422–424)

Anxious/Fearful Cluster (p. 424–427)

7. Briefly describe the three disorders in the anxious/fearful cluster. (Note how obsessive-compulsive personality disorder is different from obsessive-compulsive disorder.) Give a speculated cause for each of the three disorders. (p. 424–427)

Therapies for Personality Disorders (p. 427–432)

8. Why are therapists often not focused on therapy for personality disorders? What does the presence of these diagnoses imply for therapy prognosis? In general, how do therapists of various paradigms approach working with personality disorders? (p. 427–428)

9. Why is therapy with borderline personalities especially difficult? Describe two approaches to therapy for borderline personalities with two or three techniques of each approach. Explain what is meant by saying that the goal of therapy with personality disorders should be to change a "disorder" into a "style". (p. 428–431)

10. How effective is psychotherapy with psychopaths and why? Summarize a recent meta-analysis with (somewhat) more optimism. Identify two points about imprisonment as a treatment for psychopaths. (p. 431–432)

Self-test, Chapter 13

(* Items not covered in Study Questions.)

Multiple-choice

1. Personality disorders and Axis I disorders are related in that
    a. they cannot both be diagnosed in the same person.
    b. if both exist, the Axis I disorder is more serious.
    c. if both exist, the personality disorder is more serious.
    d. the personality disorder provides a context for the Axis I disorder.

2. A major problems that remains in diagnosing personality disorders is
    a. low reliability on retest.
    b. poor interrater reliability.
    c. unstructured diagnostic criteria.
    d. very low occurrence in the population for most of the disorders.

3. Paranoid personality disorder differs from paranoid schizophrenia in that paranoid
    personality is
    a. not associated with unreasonable paranoia.
    b. associated with different delusions than schizophrenics.
    c. not associated with thought disorder.
    d. not likely to present with depression.

*4. Borderline Personality Disorder is most associated with which factor from the five factor
    model of personality?
    a. Extroversion/introversion
    b. Openness to experience
    c. Neuroticism/antagonism
    d. Agreeableness/antagonism

5. In object relations theory, 'splitting' refers to the tendency of borderline personality
    disorders to
    a. separate themselves from society.
    b. forget unpleasant events.
    c. see people as all good or all bad.
    d. think illogically.

*6. A precursor to antisocial personality disorder is
    a. conduct disorder.
    b. oppositional disorder.
    c. antisocial disorder of childhood or adolescence.
    d. pervasive developmental disorder.

7. Cleckley emphasized which of the following aspects of antisocial personality that is not
    emphasized in DSM-IV?
    a. Acting out as a child.
    b. Lack of shame or guilt.
    c. Reckless and aggressive.
    d. Impulsive antisocial acts.

*8.   The dimensional approach to personality disorders
       a. places people into distinct categories of personality style.
       b. explains personality disorders as extremes of normal personality traits.
       c. views personality disorders as learned evolutionary behaviors.
       d. identifies personality disorders according to four key dimensions.

9.   Individuals with Borderline Personality Disorder are difficult to treat because
       a. their intellectual functioning is too low for them to reach true insights.
       b. they do not feel distressed, despite being so distressing to others.
       c. they have extreme difficulties relating to others, including a therapist.
       d. All of the above choices are correct.

10.   Dialectical behavior therapy for patients with borderline personality disorder combines
       a. social skills training and free-association.
       b. ego analysis and more directive behavioral techniques.
       c. behavioral problem-solving and client-centered empathy.
       d. gestalt techniques and relaxation training.

Short Answer

1.   Define "personality disorders" (as a group).

2.   Why are personality disorders placed on a different axis of DSM-IV-TR?

3.   Distinguish between schizoid and schizotypal personality disorders.

4.   How are histrionic and narcissistic personality disorders both the same and different?

5.   Research on the role of the family finds that psychopaths tend to come from families characterized by . . .

6.   Describe research on response modulation showing impulsivity in psychopaths.

7.   What is the (speculated) cause of obsessive-compulsive personality disorder?

8.   Marco seeks psychotherapeutic help. It's clear that he has a personality disorder as well as an Axis I problem. What is the therapeutic implication of his also having a Axis II diagnosis?

9.   What does it mean to say that the goal of therapy should be to change disorders into styles?

10. How effective is the standard treatment for psychopaths?

Answers to Self-test, Chapter 13

Multiple-choice

1. d (p. 409)   2. a (p. 410)   3. c (p. 412)   4. c (p. 414)
5. c (p. 415)   6. a (p. 418)   7. b (p. 418–419)   8. b (p. 426)
9. c (p. 428–429) 10. c (p.429)

Short Answer

1.   Characterized by enduring, inflexible patterns of inner experience and behavior that deviate from cultural expectations and cause distress or impairment. (p. 409)

2.   To remind clinicians to consider their possible presence (in addition to Axis I disorders, which are often the reason the person seeks help). (p. 410)

3.   Both have few close friends but, in addition, schizotypal personality disorder involves eccentric ideas, mannerisms, appearance, etc. (p. 412)

4.   Both are self-centered. Seemingly histrionics seek to prove they are special (seek to impress others, etc.) while narcissistics are, already, convinced they are special (deserve special attention, etc.). (p. 416–417)

5.   Rejection, lack of affection, inconsistent discipline, antisocial fathers. (p. 421)

6.   In a card game where the odds of winning decreased steadily, psychopaths continued to play (and lose) longer than others, unless they were required to wait 5 seconds before deciding whether to continue. (p. 423–424)

7.   They are overcompensating for fear of loss of control by pushing to control as much of their life as possible. (p. 427)

8.   Implication is that therapy will take longer and outcome is less optimistic as Marco has both and acute problem and an underlying, long-term, problem. (p. 427)

9.   The goal should be not to change the person's basic approach to life but to help the person express it in more adaptive, moderate, flexible ways. (p. 431)

10. The standard treatment (prison) is not very effective at all. In fact, criminologists have argued that prisons are schools for crime. (p. 432)

14 Sexual and Gender Identity Disorders

Overview

Chapter 14 is the last of three chapters on problems with a social emphasis. Generally these are not considered "mental illnesses" as such but involve particular behaviors or traits that are of concern to society and, sometimes, to the individual. Chapter 12 discussed substance abuse problems that concern both society and the individual to varying degrees. Social and individual concerns about these problems can change dramatically as has happened with cigarette smoking. Chapter 13 discussed personality disorders. Many of these, especially antisocial personality disorders, are clearly more a "problem" for society than for the individual criminal.

Chapter 14 covers sexual problems. Sexual deviations, as the term implies, refer to sexual activities that society considers deviant or aberrant. Like the personality disorders and substance abuse disorders of the last two chapters, defining a sexual activity as "deviant" involves a value judgment. Again our social and individual concerns may change as has happened regarding homosexuality. Sexual dysfunctions are much more common sexual problems involving inhibitions of sexual functioning. Sexual dysfunctions include premature orgasm, vaginismus, and inhibited sexual desire or arousal.

Chapter 14 is the last chapter focusing on socially problematic behaviors. The next two chapters discuss issues and problems of childhood (Chapter 15) and of old age (Chapter 16). Then the text concludes with two chapters on treatment and legal/ethical issues.

Chapter Summary

In *Gender Identity Disorder* individuals have a sense of themselves as being of one sex although they are, anatomically, the other sex. Such individuals may seek sex-change surgery to make their physical anatomy consistent with their inner sense of themselves. Behavior therapy can also help them change their behaviors, sexual fantasies, etc., to match their anatomy.

The Paraphilias involve unusual sexual activities or fantasies that the individual either acts on or is markedly disturbed by. They may involve sexual gratification through intimate articles, cross dressing, or through sexual activities involving pain, children, strangers, etc. Theories of paraphilias often suggest multiple ways they could develop. Behavior therapists treat such problems using aversion therapy to reduce the unwanted attraction plus social skills training to enable normal sexual relations.

Rape is more an act of violence than of sex. Many professionals view it as a result of social stereotypes. Treatment of rapists is difficult and attention focuses on helping victims cope with the trauma.

The Sexual Dysfunctions are persistent and recurrent inhibitions in sexual functioning that may develop at each stage of the human sexual response cycle. While organic factors may be involved, psychological factors are usually central. Masters and Johnson theorize that historical factors, such as early sexual teachings and experiences, may lead the individual to develop performance fears or adopt a spectator role thus inhibiting full participation in sexual activities. Therapies for sexual dysfunctions are highly effective. They focus both on sexual skills and on the relationship.

Essential Concepts

1.   Gender identity disorders involve feeling that one is the opposite of one's anatomical sex.

2.   The two major treatments for gender identity disorders (sex-change surgery and alterations in gender identity) remain controversial.

3.   Paraphilias involve a deviation in the object of sexual arousal.

4.   The more common paraphilias include fetishism, transvestic fetishism, incest, pedophilia, voyeurism, exhibitionism, sadism, and masochism.

5.   Treatment of paraphilias has focused on the behavior itself via behavioral therapy and judicial interventions. Their effectiveness is unclear and suggests a multifaceted approach is needed.

6.   Rape is often more a crime of aggression and dominance and can have a tremendously adverse impact on the victim.

7.   Sexual dysfunctions are inhibitions or disturbances in one of four phases of the human sexual response cycle.

8.   The sexual response cycle is described as having appetitive, excitement, orgasm, and resolution phases.

9.   Sexual dysfunctions include (in the appetitive phase) hypoactive sexual desire and sexual aversion; (in the excitement phase) female arousal and male erectile disorders; (in the orgasm phase) female or male orgasmic disorders, and premature ejaculation; as well as sexual pain disorders of vaginismus, and dyspareunia.

10.   Masters and Johnson proposed that historical factors lead to current factors (performance fears and the spectator role) resulting in sexual dysfunctions.

11.   Behavioral and cognitive treatments for sexual dysfunctions are very effective. They include anxiety reduction, education, frank discussion about sexuality, and specific techniques for treating dysfunctions.

Key Terms

Sexual and gender identity disorders (p. 435)

Gender identity (p. 435)

Transsexualism [Gender identity disorder — GID] (p. 435)

Sex-reassignment surgery (p. 438)

Paraphilias (p. 441)

Fetishism (p. 441)

Transvestic fetishism (p. 442)

Pedophiles (p. 442)

Incest (p. 443)

Child sexual abuse [CSA] (p. 444)

Voyeurism [peeping] (p. 444)

Exhibitionism (p. 445)

Frotteurism (p. 448)

Sexual sadism (p. 448)

Sexual masochism (p. 448)

Orgasmic reorientation (p. 452)

Forced rape (p. 454)

Statutory rape (p. 454)

Acquaintance [date] rape (p. 455)

Sexual dysfunctions (p. 460)

Homosexuality (p. 461)

Ego-dystonic homosexuality (p. 461)

Homophobia (p. 461)

Hypoactive sexual desire disorder (p. 462)

Sexual aversion disorder (p. 462)

Female sexual arousal disorder (p. 463)

Male erectile disorder (p. 463)

Female orgasmic disorder (p. 464)

Male orgasmic disorder (p. 465)

Premature ejaculation (p. 465)

Dyspareunia (p. 466)

Vaginismus (p. 466)

Fear of performance (p. 467)

Spectator role (p. 467)

Sexual value system (p. 470)

Sensate focus (p. 470)

Sensory-awareness procedures (p. 471)

Study Questions

1. Identify and distinguish among the three kinds of sexual problems discussed in this chapter. (p. 435)

Gender Identity Disorder (p. 435–441)

2. Define gender identity disorder (GID) noting it is based on inner beliefs not behavior. Summarize evidence that biological factors and social/psychological factors are (and are not) involved. How do cultural values complicate this topic? (p. 435–438)

3. Describe the steps in treating GID by altering the body. Does this treatment appear effective (and why is its effectiveness difficult to evaluate)? Describe attempts to alter gender identity and the ethical dilemma in such efforts. (p. 438–441)

The Paraphilias (p. 441–454)

4.   Define paraphilias as a group of disorders. Explain issues around the use of "recurrent" and "distressed" as part of these definitions. Define eight types of paraphilia and the background or personality factors usually associated with each. (p. 441–448)

5.   Summarize perspectives on the etiology of the paraphilias including one psychodynamic, five behavioral/cognitive, and one biological perspective. (p. 449–451)

6.   Describe two general issues in treatment of paraphilias. What has been the impact of psychoanalytic approaches? Describe a range of behavioral and cognitive treatments and their overall effectiveness. Describe biological treatments and issues in their use. Describe Megan's Law as a preventive measure and its unintended consequence. (p. 451–454)

Rape (p. 454–459)

7.   Is rape a sexual crime? Explain. What are the effects of rape on victims during and after the attack? Identify common motivations of rapists. (p. 454–458)

8.   Describe the common approach to treating rapists and its effectiveness.   What are the immediate and long-term goals in counseling rape victims? (p. 458–459)

Sexual Dysfunctions (p. 459–473)

9.   How are sexual dysfunctions different from other sexual problems discussed earlier? Describe the four phases of the human sexual response cycle. (p. 460–462)

10. How common are occasional disturbances in sexual functioning and when are they labeled dysfunctions? Describe nine sexual dysfunctions organized into four categories. (Note the parallels between these categories and the phases of the human sexual response cycle.) Identify common causes of each dysfunction. (p. 462–466)

11. According to Masters and Johnson, how do current and historical factors interact to result in sexual dysfunctions? Briefly describe their two current and seven historical factors. (p. 467–468)

12. Identify five factors suggested by other contemporary views and two general cautions regarding this area. (p. 468–469)

13. Briefly describe seven techniques used in treating sexual dysfunctions. Notice that, in practice, combinations of these techniques are used. (p. 469–473)

Self-test, Chapter 14

(* Items not covered in Study Questions.)

Multiple-choice

1. Conflicts between anatomical sex and gender identity appear linked to
   a. emphasis paid to occasional cross dressing in childhood.
   b. the desire on the part of a parent to have a child of the opposite sex.
   c. hormonal imbalances during pregnancy.
   d. gender role of the parents.

2. Successful treatment for altering gender identity in adolescents and adults has been demonstrated by which approach?
   a. Therapy emphasizing the unconscious conflicts underlying the behavior.
   b. Behavior therapy involving reinforcement for behavior associated with the traditional gender role.
   c. Cognitive therapy focused on changing maladaptive beliefs about gender.
   d. None of the above has been able to change gender identity.

3. Harvey finds women's clothing, particularly undergarments, sexually arousing. He especially enjoys watching his girlfriend undress. Which of the following DSM-IV-TR diagnoses would fit Harvey's case?
   a. fetishism
   b. transvestic fetishism
   c. voyeurism
   d. None of the above.

4. The current thinking regarding the biological theory of paraphilias suggests
   a. a strong genetic contribution.
   b. the disposition toward paraphilias resides in the limbic system.
   c. a minor role for hormonal dysregulation.
   d. biological factors are associated with alcohol use, which leads to paraphilias.

5. The most frequent case of rape involves
   a. attack by strangers.
   b. attack by strangers as part of robbery.
   c. acquaintance or date rape.
   d. rape by a family member.

6. Therapy for rape victims includes helping the victim
   a. deal with reactions of her friends and family.
   b. identify ways she could have prevented the attack.
   c. put memories behind her and get on with daily living.
   d. decide if she is strong enough to cope with stresses of a trial.

7. Which of the following DSM-IV-TR disorders is associated with the appetitive phase of the human sexual response cycle?
   a. premature ejaculation
   b. vaginismus
   c. hypoactive sexual desire disorder
   d. female sexual arousal disorder

8. Which has been offered as a possible cause of female orgasmic disorder?
   a. Trying too hard to please one's partner.
   b. Not knowing how to have orgasms.
   c. Pain during intercourse.
   d. Excessive masturbation.

9. Pain during sexual intercourse is usually caused by
   a. vaginismus.
   b. performance anxiety.
   c. problems in the marital relationship.
   d. a medical problem.

10. Dr. Karvol, a sex therapist, instructed her clients to take some time at home to give each other pleasure through touching and caressing. The couple was told to take turns touching each other, focusing only on the pleasure felt and not on achieving a particular sexual response or completing intercourse. This exercise is called
    a. enacting a spectator role.
    b. sensate focus.
    c. the stop-start method.
    d. pleasure-centered intimacy.

SHORT ANSWER

1. Why is it difficult to evaluate the effectiveness of sex change surgery for GID?

2. Define frotteurism.

3. Describe the behavioral approach to treatment of paraphilias.

4. What has been an unintended consequence of Megan's Law?

5. What are the psychological effects of rape on the victim?

6. Describe the effectiveness of therapy for rapists.

7. How are sexual dysfunctions different from other sexual problems discussed in the text?

8.   What is the "spectator role" in Masters and Johnson's theory of sexual dysfunction?

9.   Identify five factors in sexual dysfunctions suggested by other contemporary views.

10.   List a number of components of therapy for sexual dysfunctions that do *not* focus directly on sexual activity as such.

Answers to Self-test, Chapter 14

Multiple-choice

1. a (p. 437)   2. b (p. 440)   3. d (p. 441)   4. c (p. 450–451)
5. c (p. 455)   6. a (p. 458)   7. c (p. 463)   8. b (p. 465)
9. d (p. 466)   10. b (p. 470)

Short Answer

1.   Difficult as people face unique challenges in living as the other sex in addition to possible other problems before surgery. (p. 439–440)

2.   Sexual touching of an unsuspecting person. (p. 448)

3.   Procedures are tailored to the individual but often include: aversive procedures to decrease inappropriate attractions, positive conditioning of appropriate attractions, and teaching of social skills so the individual can find partners. (p. 452)

4.   People may have to publicly register as sex offenders because they were once arrested for things (like consensual gay sex) that are no longer crimes and involved no threat to others. (p. 454)

5.   Terrified, vulnerable, and violated during attack. Afterwards tense, humiliated, angry, or guilty. Nightmares, continued fears, sexual difficulties are common. (p. 455–456)

6.   Difficult to evaluate but probably somewhat lower recidivism. As with paraphilias, treatment is often attempted in prison with minimally motivated people. (p. 458)

7.   Dysfunctions are inhibitions in normal, conventional sexual activity. The other problems involve presence of unconventional sexual activity. (p. 460)

8.   Sense of being an observer, rather than a participant, during sex. That is, of being detached and thinking rather than involved and feeling. (p. 467)

9.   Dysfunctions often involve: Both sexual and interpersonal problems. Lack of knowledge/skills. Poor communication. Fears of venereal disease. Psychological problems of the individuals. (p. 469)

10. Anxiety reduction, skills and communication training, couples therapy focusing on communication issues, etc. (p. 469–472)

15 Disorders of Childhood

Overview

Chapter 14 concluded three chapters on socially problematic behaviors and traits. This is the first of two chapters devoted to developmental problems and issues. Chapter 15 covers issues and problems that arise in childhood, Chapter 16 covers issues and problems of old age. Both chapters focus on special issues of young/old people in our society as well as on their psychological problems.

Disorders of childhood (in this chapter) are complicated by several factors. Children are developing and changing rapidly. They have difficulty expressing their concerns or asking for help. Not surprisingly, they often receive help for problems that bother the adults around them. Typically these include misbehavior (hyperactivity and conduct disorders) and educational difficulties (learning disabilities and mental retardation). The chapter also covers childhood autism, a serious and pervasive developmental problem.

The next chapter, Chapter 16, will deal with problems of aging. Older individuals are subject to a wide variety of problems. They must cope with deterioration as well as whatever problems they may have developed over time. More importantly they must cope with the realization that they are getting older as well as the fact that society often does not seem to respect, value, or provide for them.

Chapters 15 and 16 complete the text's discussion of specific problems. The last chapters of the text focus on other issues related to abnormal psychology. Chapter 17 discusses issues in psychological intervention. Chapter 18 covers legal and ethical issues. Such issues have been mentioned throughout the text. The last two chapters provide a more organized and extensive discussion of them.

Chapter Summary

Classification of Childhood Disorders is complicated because, as children develop, our expectations for their behavior change.

Children with *attention-deficit/hyperactivity disorder* have trouble focusing their attention, and act impulsively leading to difficulty in school and play activities. Their diverse problems may have different causes although biological factors appear primary.

Conduct disorder involves acting-out behaviors such as juvenile delinquency. Because it can develop into adult criminality, a wide range of treatments have been developed.

Learning Disabilities are developmental delays in specific areas (reading, etc.) not related to general intellectual retardation. Research, especially on dyslexia, has suggested problems in specific brain areas. Treatment consists of teaching specific skills.

A diagnosis of *Mental Retardation* traditionally involves three criteria: subnormal intellectual functioning, deficits in adaptive behavior, and onset before age 18. Severe retardation typically results from biological causes such as chromosomal abnormalities or brain injuries. Mild retardation with no clear cause is much more common and probably results from a diverse combination of factors. Educational and behavioral programs are used to treat educational problems of retarded individuals and to improve their social functioning.

Autistic Disorder is, fortunately, an uncommon disorder in which very young children show profound problems in speech, learning, and social relations. Research has not supported early theories which suggested that autistic children had been rejected by emotionally cold parents. Biological causes are suspected. Treatment of autism is difficult. Behavioral procedures using modeling and operant conditioning are promising. However, most autistic children remain intellectually and socially limited.

Essential Concepts

1. Externalizing disorders include hyperactivity and conduct disorders.

2. Attention-deficit/hyperactivity disorder probably has biological causes and is characterized by inattention, impulsivity, overactivity, academic difficulties, and troubled peer relationships.

3. Conduct disorders can progress into adult criminality. Multiple causes appear involved and require intervention on many levels.

4. Learning disabilities are specific developmental problems in an isolated area of academic or similar functioning and are typically treated in the schools.

5. Traditional diagnostic criteria for mental retardation are: (a) significantly subaverage intellectual functioning, (b) deficits in adaptive behavior, and (c) onset prior to age 18.

6. There are four classification levels of mental retardation (mild, moderate, severe, and profound), with different IQ scores and prognoses for each level.

7. The specific etiology for most cases of mental retardation is unknown. A wide combination of biological and environmental factors is probably involved. These cases generally fall in the mild category.

8. More severe cases of mental retardation typically result from known physical causes including Down's syndrome, PKU, and various chemical and environmental hazards.

9. Public law 94-142 helped encourage a wide range of institutional and educational programs for retarded individuals to improve their behavioral, academic, and social functioning.

10. Autistic disorder is characterized by extreme aloneness, severe communication problems, and ritualistic behavior.

11. The specific etiology of infantile autism remains unknown, although research strongly suggests biological, not psychological, factors.

12. Highly structured social-learning treatments have been successful in reducing self-injury and in improving communication and self-care skills of autistic children; however, their long-term prognosis is limited.

Key Terms

Externalizing disorders (p. 476)

Internalizing disorders (p. 476)

Attention-deficit/hyperactivity disorder [ADHD] (p. 478)

Conduct disorder (p. 484)

Oppositional defiant disorder (p. 484)

Learning disabilities (p. 492)

Learning disorders (p. 492)

Reading disorder [dyslexia] (p. 492)

Disorder of written expression (p. 493)

Mathematics disorder (p. 493)

Expressive language disorder (p. 493)

Phonological disorder (p. 493)

Stuttering (p. 493)

Motor skills disorder (p. 493)

Enuresis (p. 494)

Mild mental retardation (p. 500)

Moderate mental retardation (p. 500)

Severe mental retardation (p. 500)

Profound mental retardation (p. 500)

Down syndrome [trisomy 21] (p. 502)

Fragile X syndrome (p. 502)

Phenylketonuria (p. 503)

Applied behavior analysis (p. 505)

Self-instructional training (p. 505)

Autistic disorder (p. 506)

Pervasive developmental disorders (p. 507)

Echolalia (p. 510)

Pronoun reversal (p. 510)

Study Questions

Classification of Childhood Disorders (p. 476–478)

1. To classify abnormal behavior in children, what must diagnosticians consider first and why? Define two broad classes into which many childhood disorders are organized. (p. 476–478)

Attention–Deficit/Hyperactivity Disorder (p. 478–484)

2. Distinguish between attention-deficit/hyperactivity disorder (ADHD) and "rambunctious kid". Identify four or so characteristics of ADHD. Distinguish between ADHD and conduct disorder. What is the adult prognosis for ADHD children? (p. 478–481)

3. Describe and evaluate the importance of biological, prenatal, environmental, and psychological factors in hyperactivity. Describe medication and psychological treatments for hyperactivity and results of studies comparing them. (p. 481–484)

Conduct Disorder (p. 484–492)

4.   Define conduct disorder and its possible relation to oppositional defiant disorder (ODD). Describe the prognosis for conduct-disordered children and efforts to predict which of them will become anti-social adults. (p. 484–487)

5.   Identify important biological, psychological, peer, and sociological influences in the etiology of conduct disorder. Describe and evaluate treatment approaches based on: incarceration, family intervention, multisystem treatment, anger-control, and moral reasoning skills. (p. 487–492)

Learning Disabilities (p. 492–498)

6.   Define seven learning disabilities in three groups. In the etiology of dyslexia, describe four possible factors (including reversing letters). In the etiology of mathematics disorder, describe three subtypes. Describe two common approaches to intervention and a common need in any intervention program. (p. 492–498)

Mental Retardation (p. 498–506)

7.   Define "mental retardation" using three traditional criteria.   Identify four levels of retardation in DSM-IV-TR including the IQ range and expected level of social functioning for each.   Describe the approach encouraged by the American Association of Mental Retardation. (p. 498–501)

8.   What percentage of retarded individuals have no clearly defined etiology? Identify typical intellectual and social characteristics of those with no identifiable etiology. For those with known etiologies, briefly describe five biological causes with an example of each. (p. 501–504)

9.   Describe and evaluate four approaches to preventing and/or treating mental retardation. (p. 501–506)

Autistic Disorder (p. 506–517)

10.   What is considered the fundamental symptom of autistic disorder? How do autistic and retarded individuals compare on IQ tests? Describe several characteristics of autism in each of three areas. What is the prognosis for autistic children? (p. 506–511)

11.   Summarize two early psychological approaches to autism. How well has research supported them? Describe results in two research areas suggesting a biological basis for infantile autism. (p. 511–515)

12.   Identify four special problems in treating autistic children. Describe and evaluate three general approaches to treating autism. (p. 515–517)

Self-test, Chapter 15

(* Items not covered in Study Questions.)

Multiple-choice

1. Externalizing problems are more frequent in _____, and internalizing problems are more frequent in _____, regardless of culture.
    a. boys: girls
    b. girls: boys
    c. boys: boys
    d. Gender distribution varies widely in different cultures.

2. If you knew that a child on a playground had ADHD, but you did not know which one, you
    a. would be able to immediately pick that child out.
    b. could only identify that child after an outburst.
    c. would have difficulty distinguishing the child from all the others.
    d. would observe a child playing alone, away from the group.

*3. Girls with ADHD
    a. are more depressed than girls without ADHD.
    b. show deficits in planning and problem-solving.
    c. are more likely to be adopted than girls without ADHD.
    d. all of the above choices are correct.

4. Which of the following is *not* a symptom of oppositional-defiant disorder?
    a. Fighting
    b. Temper tantrums
    c. Refusing to follow directions
    d. Annoying others deliberately

5. According to Dodge and Frame (1982), aggressive children demonstrate cognitive biases in situations
    a. in which peers act aggressively.
    b. in which peers act in a prosocial manner.
    c. which are ambiguous.
    d. in which they are rejected.

*6. Typically, the outcome for stuttering is
    a. complete recovery, even without intervention.
    b. recovery to the point that the person only stutters when nervous.
    c. complete recovery is possible if speech therapy is initiated early.
    d. most people do not recover, even with speech therapy.

7. Which of the following self-care skills would be difficult for an adult with *mild* mental retardation?
    a. bathing
    b. dressing
    c. eating
    d. None of the above.

8.   What term is used to describe the following communication: Mother: "Would you like to play with this?" Child: "Would you like to play with this?"
     a. pronoun reversal
     b. echolalia
     c. alogia
     d. extreme autistic aloneness

9.   Autistic disorder was originally attributed to
     a. emotionally cold parenting.
     b. birth trauma.
     c. food allergies.
     d. child abuse.

10. The most common medication prescribed for autism is
     a. antipsychotic medication.
     b. stimulant medication.
     c. antidepressants.
     d. drugs which lower serotonin levels.

Short Answer

1.   What issue must be considered before diagnosing any childhood disorder and why?

2.   Distinguish between ADHD and "rambunctious kid".

3.   How effective are drug treatments for hyperactivity?

4.   What has been found by studies on which children with conduct disorder will grow up to become anti-social adults?

5.   Describe what is done in family intervention with conduct-disordered children.

6.   Summarize the evidence regarding visual perceptual deficits as a basis for dyslexia.

7.   Describe the approach to measuring mental retardation which is encouraged by the American Association of Mental retardation.

8.   Describe PKU as a cause of mental retardation.

9.   Describe what is done in cognitive interventions for treating mental retardation.

10.   What research suggests a genetic basis for autism?

Answers to Self-test, Chapter 15

Multiple-choice

1. a (p. 477)   2. c (p. 478)   3. d (p. 480)   4. a (p. 484)
5. c (p. 488)   6. a (p. 493)   7. d (p. 500)   8. b (p. 510)
9. a (p. 512–513)   10. a (p. 517)

Short Answer

1. What behavior is normal for the age. The "symptoms" may be common for the child's age. (p. 476)

2. Many kids are active and rambunctious. ADHD is for extreme and persistent problems, not just kids who are more active than parents or teachers prefer. (p. 478)

3. Drugs improve concentration and reduce behavior problems but have little effect on long-term academic achievement and have side-effects. (p. 483)

4. Some success in identifying children likely to continue into adulthood with severe problems but less success in predicting those who will out grow problems. Predictors include IQ and antisocial behavior in parents. (p. 486–487)

5. Parental behavior management training emphasizing positive reinforcement of prosocial behavior plus time-outs, etc. for misbehavior. (p. 489)

6. Research has not supported past theories linking dyslexia to perceptual deficits such as seeing letters backwards. (p. 494)

7. Measure strengths and weaknesses in terms of support or remediation needed to achieve higher functioning. (p. 500–501)

8. PKU is a genetic inability to process phenylalanine, an amino acid. Without special diet phenylalanine accumulates in the body, producing brain damage and retardation. (p. 503)

9. Children are taught to verbalize and carry out cognitive steps to solve problems. Teacher verbalizes cognitions while solving, then verbalizes while child solves, then child verbalizes while solves, etc. (p. 505–506)

10. Risk of autism rises dramatically in siblings of autistic children; up to 91% in identical twins of autistics. (Cannot do family studies as autistics rarely marry.) (p. 514)

16 Aging and Psychological Disorders

Overview

Chapter 16 is the concluding chapter on developmental problems. Chapter 15 discussed disorders of childhood and growing up. Chapter 16 is devoted to the problems of aging and growing old. Both young and old people in our society are vulnerable. Others do not always think about their special circumstances and needs or provide care and attention they may need. This is more true for older than for younger people — a disturbing thought for those who plan to live long enough to grow old.

Chapter 16 completes the text's discussion of specific psychological disorders. The last two chapters of the text deal more intensively with issues in abnormal psychology. Chapter 17 evaluates various treatment methods and discusses issues integrating them. Finally, Chapter 18 will cover legal and ethical issues. Legal issues include issues regarding the insanity defense and commitment of disturbed individuals. Ethical issues cover rights of therapy clients and research participants. Earlier chapters have mentioned these topics in various contexts. The last two chapters bring together and complete these discussions.

Chapter Summary

Growing old is, obviously, a time of physical decline. Medical problems become an increasing concern. Beyond the purely medical aspects of old age, however, are a wide range of psychological and social problems.

The chapter begins by summarizing *Issues, Concepts, and Methods in the Study of Older Adults*. This discussion forms a basis for considering physical and psychological disorders of older adults.

Old Age and Brain Disorders covers two disorders: dementias are slowly developing, progressive conditions that are usually irreversible and require supportive care. Deliriums develop suddenly and, if recognized, can often be reversed by treating the underlying physical conditions.

Old Age and Psychological Disorders emphasizes factors that make older adults more (or less) susceptible to various problems. Depression often accompanies physical and psychological declines as people grow old. Anxiety problems may continue from younger years or develop as new issues emerge. Suspiciousness and paranoia may result as older people have difficulty understanding others due to hearing problems and social isolation. Older adults are also subject to other psychological problems. For example, suicide may result as they struggle to accept changing physical and social situations. Contrary to popular conceptions, older adults are capable of enjoying and engaging in sexual activity despite slowed biological responses.

Treatment and Care of Older Adults is complicated by stereotypes and misinformation among professionals. Nursing homes and other facilities often fail to encourage older adults to maintain their skills and capabilities. Community-based services could help older people remain as independent as possible.

Issues Specific to Therapy with Older Adults include changing social and personal realities. Therapists can adjust the content and process of therapy to reflect these issues.

Essential Concepts

1. Age effects, cohort effects, and time-of-measurement effects complicate research efforts to understand older adults.

2. Dementia is a gradual deterioration of intellectual abilities over several years until functioning becomes impaired.

3. Many cases of dementia are irreversible. Treatment consists of support and assistance in living as independently as possible.

4. Most dementia patients are in the care of their families and support for these families is valuable, especially when they must decide about institutionalization.

5. Delirium is a clouded state of consciousness characterized by difficulty in concentrating and maintaining a directed stream of thought. Many cases of delirium are reversible if detected in time.

6. There is a tendency to attribute the behavior of older adults to the fact that they are older. This can lead to erroneous conclusions about the effects of aging and cause us to overlook the individual's uniqueness.

7. Difficulties of growing old can contribute to psychological problems including depression, paranoid disorder, abuse of prescription drugs, and insomnia.

8. Most older adults maintain sexual interest and engage in sexual activity although there may be a general slowing of the sexual response cycle and the intensity of sexual arousal may not be as great.

9. Regardless of whether they are cared for in the community or in a nursing home, giving the aged responsibility for self-care, planning, and control over their lives is important to their continued psychological and physical well-being.

10. Psychotherapy with older adults requires sensitivity to their special issues. They can benefit from help in coping with the realistic problems of old age.

Key Terms

Ageism (p. 520)

Age effects (p. 522)

Cohort effects (p. 522)

Time of measurement effects (p. 522)

Cross-sectional studies (p. 522)

Longitudinal studies (p. 522)

Selective mortality (p. 523)

Dementia (p. 524)

Alzheimer's disease (p. 525)

Plaques (p. 525)

Neurofibrillary tangles (p. 525)

Delirium (p. 531)

Paraphrenia (p. 541)

Sleep apnea (p. 547)

Study Questions

Issues, Concepts, and Methods in the Study of Older Adults (p. 522–524)

1. How does diversity change as people age? Identify three effects that influence research on aging. Describe two factors that complicate both cross-sectional and longitudinal studies of older adults. How justified is the DSM approach to psychopathology in later life?. (p. 522–524)

Old Age and Brain Disorders (p. 524–534)

2. Define two forms of brain disorder that may affect older people (on p. 524 and 531). Describe common symptoms and the common cause of dementia in older adults. What are the physiological changes and genetic factors in Alzheimer's? Describe the goals of biological treatment and of psychosocial treatment directed toward the patient and toward caregivers. (p. 524–531)

3. Describe common symptoms of delirium and distinguish them from symptoms of dementia. What are common causes and treatment? (p. 531–534)

Old Age and Psychological Disorders (p. 534–553)

4.   Why do we tend to ignore psychological problems among older adults — and how common are they? (p. 534–535) List the nine psychological problems covered on pages 535–553.

5.   The text describes depression, anxiety, and delusional (paranoid) disorders. For each problem describe (a) how it differs in older people, (b) possible causes, and (c) treatment. (p. 535–541)

6.   Briefly describe two or three issues for each of the following topics (a) schizophrenia, (b) alcohol abuse, (c) abuse of illegal drugs, and (d) medication misuse in older adults. (p. 541–546)

7.   Describe the causes and treatment of three other psychological problems among older people. (p. 546–550)

8.   How does sexuality change with age? Describe physiological changes for men and for women as well as general problems related to age. What is the general approach to treating sexual dysfunctions in older people? (p. 550–553)

Treatment and Care of Older Adults (p. 553–559)

9.   Identify three common misperceptions that limit treatment of older adults. (p. 553)

10. What are common effects of nursing home placement on family caregivers? Summarize a study suggesting subtle problems in nursing home care and possible reasons for the results. Identify two other reasons for poor physical and mental health care. (p. 554–557)

11. Describe alternative living settings. Describe community-based care and three problems in caring for older people in the community. (p. 557–559)

Issues Specific to Therapy with Older Adults (p. 559–562)

12. Identify six content and six process issues in providing therapy to older adults. (p. 559–562)

Self-test, Chapter 16

(* Items not covered in Study Questions.)

Multiple-choice

1. Which of the following statements is an example of an age effect?
    a. Today's older adults are less likely to seek mental health services because when they were growing up, mental illness was stigmatized.
    b. Because exercise has become widely promoted in the media, many older adults are now exercising and thus healthier than was predicted by earlier measures of their physical well-being.
    c. Because of the effects of aging on the brain, older adults do less well than younger adults on measures of academic performance.
    d. In a longitudinal study, many of the elderly subjects died before the follow-up data was collected.

2. A lay term for dementia is
    a. CVA.
    b. stroke.
    c. delirium.
    d. senility.

3. Treatment of delirium consists primarily of
    a. support and assistance to maintain functioning as long as possible.
    b. institutionalization to lower stress and reduce accident risks.
    c. prescribing drugs to manage symptoms.
    d. identifying and treating the underlying cause.

4. Which of the following is true regarding psychological disorders in the elderly?
    a. Prevalence of mental disorders increases with age.
    b. Complaints (but not prevalence) increase with age.
    c. Cognitive impairments are the most common problem.
    d. Most disorders are not amenable to psychotherapy.

5. Which of the following is *most* common in the elderly?
    a. abuse of illegal drugs
    b. abuse of legal medications
    c. alcohol abuse
    d. paraphrenia

6. Unlike younger adults, older adults commit suicide for
    a. alleviation of personal distress.
    b. philosophical reasons, such as reduction of family burden.
    c. narcissistic reasons, such as due to a personal insult.
    d. reduction of anxiety.

7. Why do women tend to have less sexual activity in old age than men?
    a. They have greater decline in their sexual functioning.
    b. They are less likely to have a sexual partner.
    c. They have a greater decrease in sexual desire.
    d. All of the above are correct.

8.   An alternative to nursing home placement that has emerged *most* recently is
       a. in home help.
       b. homes that are adjacent, physically, to inpatient hospitals.
       c. specially equipped homes tailor-made to the physical needs of the elderly.
       d. assisted living settings.

9.   As social anxiety increases in the elderly
       a. physical and psychological health increase.
       b. women's well-being increases, but it is unrelated to men's well-being.
       c. women's well-being is unaffected, but men's well-being increases.
       d. there is an increased focus upon only a few close friends.

10.   Which of the following is a recommended content issue in therapy with older adults?
       a. Encouraging clients to make new social contacts.
       b. Helping clients deal directly with fear of death.
       c. Not attributing personal problems to medical or social problems.
       d. Keeping up spirits despite difficulties.

Short Answer

1.   Are older people more similar or more different from each other compared to younger people? Explain briefly.

2.   Your older friend seems confused. What behavioral differences would help you determine if your friend is experiencing delirium or dementia?

3.   You are a psychotherapist assigned to work with an older person with Alzheimer's. What would you emphasize in working with them?

4.   List some symptoms of depression which are especially common in older depressed adults.

5.   What are common causes of paranoia in older adults?

6.   What is the general approach to treating sexual dysfunctions in older adults?

7.   Identify three general issues in psychological treatment and care of older adults.

8.   Summarize a study suggesting that even good-quality nursing home care may be undesirable.

9.   Identify three problems in caring for older people in the community.

10.   Explain "life review" as an issue in therapy with older adults.

Answers to Self-test, Chapter 16

Multiple-choice

1. c (p. 522)	2. d (p. 524)	3. d (p. 533)	4. c (p. 534–535)
5. b (p. 545–546)	6. b (p. 549)	7. b (p. 551)	8. d (p. 555–557)
9. d (p. 559)	10. b (p. 560)		

Short Answer

1.   Despite stereotypes, older people are more diverse than younger. (p. 522)

2.   Delirium tends to have rapid onset, not just forgetful but overtly confused thinking and speech, bewildered, sleep-wake cycles disrupted, nightmares and hallucinations more likely. (p. 524, 531)

3.   Emphasize gentle reassurance (possibly life review). Not seek to provide insight into problem or seek major psychological changes. (p. 529)

4.   Depressed older adults are more likely to have somatic complaints, slowed motor behavior, weight loss, and physical decline. Less common generally are cognitive and emotional symptoms. (p. 535–536)

5.   Results from attempts to fill in gaps in understanding caused by memory or sensory losses, social isolation, etc. especially in people with a history of suspiciousness. (p. 540–541)

6.   Treated the same way as for younger people, although with special consideration for physical changes and limits, and remembering that sex was a taboo topic when they grew up. Educate on changes with aging. (p. 552–553)

7.   Professionals are less likely to notice, refer problems. They have lower expectations for improvement. This despite older adults being more thoughtful and thus, seemingly, more amenable to therapy. (p. 553)

8.   Old people were randomly assigned to three intensities of professional care. Results showed that more professional involvement increased death rates because the professionals pushed nursing home placement (where early death was more likely). (p. 554)

9.   Coordinating services among many agencies with various rules. Health care professionals don't enjoy working with problems of older people. Conflicts with family members who feel angry, guilty, etc. over care issues. (p. 557–559)

10.   Older people often seek, and may benefit from, reviewing their lives and considering the meaning and implications of their lives and experiences. (p. 561)

17 Outcomes and Issues in Psychological Intervention

Overview

The previous chapter completed the text's discussion of major forms of abnormal behavior. Chapter 17 begins the last section of the text, which covers issues in abnormal psychology. These issues underlie many topics covered earlier and round out discussion of the field.

Chapter 17 discusses issues in psychological intervention. Psychological interventions for various disorders were covered in the chapters on those disorders. Chapter 17 brings these interventions together and discusses efforts to integrate them. Chapter 18 deals with legal and ethical issues. Legal issues include insanity, competency to stand trial, and involuntary commitment. Ethical issues concern the rights of research participants and therapy clients.

Chapter Summary

Chapter 17 is devoted to evaluating, comparing, and integrating psychological interventions. Many of these approaches to psychological treatment were introduced in earlier chapters.

General Issues in Evaluating Psychotherapy Research discusses the related but different goals of psychotherapy researchers seeking to conduct quality research and psychotherapists seeking to help individuals in the real world.

Review of Psychoanalytic Therapies summarizes therapy approaches growing out of Freud's work. Classical psychoanalysis focuses on repressed childhood conflicts while briefer analytic approaches focus more on current life issues. Evaluations of these approaches have looked at both theoretical issues and research on their effectiveness.

Review of Client-Centered Therapy covers Carl Rogers' approach. Rogers originated the field of psychotherapy research and his model has shown modest effectiveness. *Review of Gestalt Therapy* discusses the similar, but more technique-oriented Gestalt approach which has been less studied.

Review of Behavioral and Cognitive Therapies reviews and evaluates counterconditioning, operant, and cognitive therapies. These approaches, growing out of research traditions, have been more clearly defined and studied in recent years. For example, Ellis' and Beck's cognitive approaches have been extensively studied and compared. Other issues in this area include questions of how to generalize and maintain therapy gains. Generally these approaches have shown considerable effectiveness and raise significant issues for the field.

Review of Couples and Family Therapy and *Review of Community Psychology* reviews these two other approaches to intervention and issues in their use.

Psychotherapy Integration discusses efforts to bring together the various approaches. Wachtel's classic effort to integrate psychoanalysis and behavior therapy illustrates how seemingly disparate approaches to therapy can benefit from each other's ideas. Integration can occur at many levels however premature integration could confuse the concepts and techniques which make various approaches valuable.

Cultural and Racial Factors in Psychological Intervention closes the chapter by reemphasizing the need to be aware of cultural differences in therapy with individuals from different backgrounds.

Essential Concepts

1. Psychological interventions can be evaluated in terms of both their theoretical assumptions and their empirical effectiveness.

2. Research is essential to evaluate and improve psychotherapy. However, research needs for standardization differ from therapist needs to individualize therapy for each client.

3. Classic psychoanalysis (which seeks to lift childhood repressions) and briefer psychodynamic therapies (focusing more on current life issues) are difficult to evaluate. The nature of "insight" and "therapeutic relationship" raises important, complex issues. Generally, research shows inconsistent to modest benefits.

4. Client-centered therapy assumes that, by valuing clients and understanding their perspective, therapists create conditions in which clients can find their own answers and goals. Psychotherapy research originated in client centered therapy and has shown its benefits generally, although core assumptions of the theory remain unclear.

5. Gestalt therapists have developed many powerful techniques but resist formal evaluation of their effectiveness.

6. Behavioral and cognitive approaches have led to a wide range of therapy techniques.

7. Counterconditioning techniques (based on classical conditioning) have proven effective with a wide range of problems. Operant techniques have also been effective, especially with children.

8. Cognitive therapists propose that actions (and problems) result from the way people make sense out of their world. Cognitive therapists include Ellis and Beck.

9. Ellis seeks to convince clients that their irrational assumptions lead to difficulties. Research supports his approach in some cases, although deciding what assumptions are "irrational" becomes ethically complex. Beck encourages people to examine the evidence for their assumptions and has shown success, although the way in which his methods lead to change is unclear.

10. Cognitive and behavioral therapies have paid special attention to how therapy progress can be generalized and maintained after therapy ends.

11.   Cognitive and behavioral therapies are more subtle than is initially obvious. They address many historical issues in psychology and, in practice, utilize a range of approaches to effect change.

12.   Couples and family therapists use a wide range of approaches to address communication problems that develop in long-term relationships. They have shown significant results although pragmatic issues remain.

13.   Community psychology seeks to prevent problems in populations. Doing so is a challenge and is difficult to evaluate. This approach grew out of, and continues to reflect, the social activism issues of the 1960s.

14.   Integration of various interventions remains a challenge. Wachtel has proposed integrating psychoanalysis and behavioral therapies. He emphasizes that current behaviors may both reflect and maintain childhood issues in a cyclical manner and that each theory can benefit from the methods and emphases of the other.

15.   Integration of psychotherapy schools can occur on many levels. Premature attempts at integration can also blur useful concepts and techniques of the various schools.

16.   Cultural and racial differences can confuse understanding and limit communication between therapist and client.

Key Terms

Efficacy (p. 567)

Effectiveness (p. 567)

Stepped care (p. 568)

Therapeutic [working] alliance (p. 573)

Triadic reciprocality (p. 583)

Paradoxical intentions (p. 586)

Reactance (p. 586)

Multimodal therapy (p. 591)

Technical eclecticism (p. 600)

Common factorism (p. 600)

Theoretical integration (p. 600)

Study Questions

General Issues in Evaluating Psychotherapy Research (p. 565–569)

1.   How have therapy manuals improved randomized clinical trials — but made them more different from therapy practice? Identify two limitations of these trials. Explain how the more idiographic approach of practitioners may be an advantage and a disadvantage. Describe two ways that managed care is using research results and the (possible) problem with each. (p. 565–569)

Review of Psychoanalytic Therapies (p. 569–574)

2.   Describe three basic concepts in classical psychoanalysis. Briefly identify five general issues in the evaluation of classical psychoanalysis. Describe four conclusions of research on classical psychoanalysis. (p. 569–572)

3. Evaluate brief psychodynamic therapies by summarizing the results of outcome research and three areas of process research. (p. 572–574)

Review of Client-Centered Therapy (p. 574–576)

4. Summarize the basic concepts of client-centered therapy in about three points. Evaluate client-centered therapy by describing research on therapist qualities, outcome, and four theoretical problems. (p. 574–576)

Review of Gestalt Therapy (p. 576)

5. Why has little research been done on Gestalt therapy? Summarize the basic concepts of Gestalt therapy in about three points and evaluate it in two points. (p. 576)

Review of Behavioral and Cognitive Therapies (p. 577–592)

6.   In general, how do behavioral and cognitive methods approach therapy?   Evaluate counterconditioning and exposure methods by describing this approach and its effectiveness in about three points.   Evaluate operant methods by describing this approach to therapy and the range of problems for which it has been effective. (p. 577–578)

7.   Evaluate cognitive behavior therapy (Ellis' and Beck's approaches) by describing their approaches and general effectiveness.   What is the issue of ethics in Ellis' approach? Compare these approaches by describing three differences and one similarity.   Summarize six additional reflections on cognitive behavior therapy. (p. 578–584)

8.   What is meant by "generalization and maintenance of treatment effects"?   Identify five ways cognitive and behavioral therapists encourage these goals.   Summarize the text's views on five basic issues in cognitive and behavior therapy. (p. 584–592)

Review of Couples and Family Therapy (p. 592–595)

9. What concept underlies all couples and family therapies? Evaluate these approaches by describing (a) their general effectiveness and (b) predictors of good and poor outcomes. (p. 592–595)

Review of Community Psychology (p. 596–597)

10. What is the basic goal of community psychology? Identify three reasons community psychology is difficult to evaluate. Summarize two political factors that contributed to the development of community psychology and two ongoing issues in the field. (p. 596–597)

Psychotherapy Integration (p. 597–602)

11. Summarize Wachtel's view on integrating psychoanalysis and behavior therapy by describing (a) his principal position, (b) a way analysts can benefit from behaviorism, and (b) four things behavior therapists can learn from psychoanalysts. (p. 597–599)

12. Identify three general ways in which psychotherapy approaches can be integrated. Summarize the text's concerns about premature integration (especially that theoretical integration may blur useful distinctions while technical eclecticism may not). (p. 599–601)

Cultural and Racial Factors in Psychological Intervention (p. 602–606)

13. Why are cultural and racial factors especially important in psychotherapy? Identify several factors affecting therapy with each of four minority groups. How can recognizing these differences contribute to a more complete science of behavior? (p. 602–606)

Self-test, Chapter 17

(* Items not covered in Study Questions.)

Multiple-choice

1. Large numbers of people are needed when conducting a randomized clinical trial
    a. to account for the various differences between groups.
    b. to protect against typically high drop-out rates which can ruin the study.
    c. because scientists are convinced only when a therapeutic effect is shown in a large number of subjects.
    d. All of the above.

*2. Todd is in therapy with an ego-analyst. A major focus of therapy will be upon
    a. unconscious conflicts between the id and ego.
    b. conscious events that become incorporated into the unconscious.
    c. Todd's ability to influence the world around him.
    d. identifying the cause of Todd's difficulties from his childhood.

3. Who is credited as originating the field of psychotherapy research?
    a. Freud
    b. Kraepelin
    c. Rogers
    d. Perls

4. Rational-Emotive Behavior Therapy has been shown to be effective for all of the following problems *except*
    a. test anxiety.
    b. development of childhood behavior problems.
    c. excessive anger.
    d. bulimia nervosa.

5. "Hot cognitions" are
    a. emotionally charged.
    b. of the greatest importance in an individual's treatment.
    c. inaccessible by the patient.
    d. based upon the perception of others.

6. Dr. Lackey conducted a study comparing the outcome of medication and therapy in treating panic disorder. At the end of the study, both groups reported a 50% reduction in their panic frequency. At one-year follow up, the medication group maintained this benefit while the therapy group reported and additional 25% reduction in panic frequency. This is an example of
    a. high external validity.
    b. placebo effects.
    c. delayed emergence of effects.
    d. stunted progress.

*7.   As part of therapy, Shauna begins to experience control over purging by only purging
       following lunch, rather than at random. Her _____ was increased in therapy.
       a. symptom
       b. reactance
       c. assertion
       d. self-efficacy

8.   Fred and Jana seek couples therapy. They will do best in treatment if
       a. Fred is depressed.
       b. one is anxious regarding treatment outcome for the relationship.
       c. they are seen for treatment together.
       d. they do not have children.

9.   Community psychology, unlike other forms of therapy, focuses upon
       a. seeking those who most need therapy.
       b. those who seek therapy.
       c. political activism as a means of accomplishing community change.
       d. YAVIS clients.

10.   Yoshi is receiving therapy for social phobia. As part of therapy, he is instructed to imitate
       a series of target behaviors demonstrated by his therapist. Yoshi will be best able to model
       these behaviors if
       a. the therapist is opposite sex.
       b. his symptoms are mild.
       c. the therapist has a similar cultural background.
       d. all of these are correct.

Short Answer

1.   In evaluating classical psychoanalysis, explain the issue regarding truthfulness of insights.

2.   In the evaluation of brief psychoanalysis, what is a "therapeutic of working alliance" and
       how important is it?

3.   What are characteristics of healthy people according to Carl Rogers' client-centered
       therapy?

4.   What does the text conclude about the therapist qualities emphasized by Rogers?

5.   Why do existential therapists reject scientific evaluation of their approach?

6.   In general, how do behavioral and cognitive methods approach therapy?

7.   Explain the ethical issue underlying irrationality in Ellis' REBT system.

8.   Summarize two ongoing issues in the field of community psychology.

9.   Summarize Wachtel's view on how to integrate psychoanalysis and behavior therapy.

10.   Why does the text argue against premature integration of psychotherapy approaches?

Answers to Self-test, Chapter 17

Multiple-choice

1. a (p. 556)   2. c (p. 570)   3. c (p. 575)   4. d (p. 578–579)
5. a (p. 583)   6. c (p. 585–586)   7. d (p. 586–587)   8. c (p. 592)
9. a (p. 596–597)   10. c (p. 602)

Short Answer

1. Insights are not verifiably "true". They are only different, hopefully better, ways of understanding ones own behavior. Thus they should be judged on whether they lead to better functioning, not on their accuracy. (p. 571)

2. Term refers to the rapport, trust, and sense of working together between therapist and client. Research indicates that a good alliance leads to good outcomes. (p. 573)

3. Rogers says healthy people are aware of their own desires and fears. They recognize and pursue their own goals. That is, they march to the beat of their own drum. (p. 575)

4. Concludes it is useful for clinicians to develop such qualities but research does not prove that simply having them is sufficient to produce change. (p. 575)

5. They consider science dehumanizing, especially when applied to individuals and their unique problems. (p. 576)

6. Approach therapy using the methods, approaches, and results of experimental psychology. (p. 577)

7. Nondistressed people likely also hold beliefs that are, strictly speaking, irrational. Ellis has made an ethical decision about what beliefs are desirable. (p. 579)

8. The field seeks social change but it is not clear (a) how to do so and (b) how to decide what changes to seek, especially when social or ethical values are involved. (p. 597)

9. He holds that present problematic behaviors both reflect and maintain childhood conflicts. That is, childhood conflicts contribute to our present behavior and, in turn, results of our present behavior reinforce the conflict. (p. 598)

10. We could lose important theoretical distinctions and, thus, treatment options. Distinctions may be issues that need to be studied and, perhaps someday, integrated, not just blurred over. (p. 600–601)

18 Legal and Ethical Issues

Overview

The last section of the text consists of two chapters discussing issues in abnormal psychology. The previous chapter covered issues in psychological intervention. It reviewed approaches to intervention and attempts to integrate them. This, the final chapter of the text, turns to legal and ethical issues in abnormal psychology. In studying this chapter, remember that "issues" do not have easy solutions — or they wouldn't be issues. Especially in working with human beings, there are often no easy answers. Thus it is important for psychologists to anticipate when issues will exist and to understand the various aspects, implications, and options involved in order to handle them as effectively as possible.

Chapter Summary

Psychologists struggle with many legal and ethical issues or dilemmas. Legal issues develop when an individual's mental condition becomes an issue in court.

In *Criminal Commitment* cases, issues develop when individuals accused of crimes are found incompetent to stand trial or are acquitted by reason of insanity at the time of the crime.

In *Civil Commitment* cases, individuals not accused of crimes may be committed to institutions if they are considered mentally ill and dangerous to themselves or others. Debate continues on whether these legal procedures are fair to the individuals involved and to larger society. Recent court rulings have clarified the legal rights of committed individuals, especially those civilly committed. These include rights to be treated in the least restrictive environment possible, to actually receive treatment, and to refuse treatment in some cases. Debate continues on how to protect individual freedoms while protecting society from disturbed individuals. Recent laws regarding released sexual offenders are an example of this debate.

Ethical Dilemmas in Therapy and Research cover a very broad area of individual rights. For example, psychologists recognize ethical obligations to obtain the informed consent of others before involving them in research and treatment. Yet research participants may not truly understand the risks involved or feel free to object. Disturbed patients, under pressure from family and society, may not be able to choose freely or even to understand the consequences of their decisions. Therapists are also ethically and legally obligated to respect the confidentiality of their patients, yet they may have to break confidentiality if, for example, patients are endangering themselves or others. Other dilemmas arise when therapy clients recover memories of childhood abuse. Such problems are true ethical dilemmas that do not always have easy answers.

Essential Concepts

1. Criminal commitment applies to individuals suspected of being mentally ill and of breaking laws while civil commitment procedures apply to individuals suspected of being mentally ill and dangerous.

2. The insanity defense deals with an individual's mental state at the time of a crime. Criteria of insanity continue to evolve and to be controversial.

3. Competency deals with an individual's mental state at the time of trial. It also raises difficult issues.

4. Laws on civil commitment vary but, generally, a person can be committed if they are (a) mentally ill and (b) a danger to themselves or others.

5. There is debate as to how accurately mental health professionals can predict a mentally disturbed individual's potential for dangerous behavior in the future.

6. Legal rulings have addressed the rights of people committed through criminal and civil proceedings. These include the right to care in the least restrictive alternate setting, the right to treatment (not just minimal custodial care), and the right to refuse especially dangerous or noxious treatments.

7. Deinstitutionalization has been an effort to get committed people out of mental hospitals. Unfortunately, it has led to other problems including homelessness.

8. Psychologists also face difficult ethical dilemmas in dealing with research participants and patients.

9. Regulations have been formulated to protect the rights of subjects in psychological research, such as the concept of informed consent — informing the subject of the risks involved in the research and of their right to freely accept or reject participation in the experiment.

10. The ethical codes of various mental health professions dictate that communications between patient and therapist must be confidential (with certain exceptions). Privileged communication laws extend this protection into the courts.

11. Therapists face additional ethical dilemmas in determining who is the client whose interests they should serve, what the goals for treatment should be, and what techniques may be justified to achieve those goals.

12. Recently therapists have confronted additional dilemmas with clients who recover memories of abuse. Protecting rights of both the alleged victim and perpetrator is complex.

Key Terms

Criminal commitment (p. 608)

Civil commitment (p. 608)

Insanity defense (p. 608)

Irresistible impulse (p. 609)

M'Naghten rule (p. 609)

Outpatient commitment (p. 624)

Advanced directive (p. 634–635)

Informed consent (p. 639)

Confidentiality (p. 641)

Privileged communication (p. 641)

Study Questions

Criminal Commitment (p. 608–621)

1. What legal assumption underlies the insanity defense? Trace the history of the insanity defense using four landmark cases and guidelines. Describe the two laws that govern most current cases. (p. 608–614)

2. Give three general points regarding insanity and mental illness. As an illustration, summarize the case of *Jones v. United States* and the Supreme Court's decision. Critique their decision by explaining three additional problems with the concept of legal insanity. (p. 614–617)

3.   Distinguish between "insanity" and "competency". What are the legal grounds on which competency is evaluated? What are the consequences of being found incompetent and the issues underlying "synthetic sanity". Explain the issue of insanity and capital punishment and illustrate its implications. (p. 614–621)

Civil Commitment (p. 621–637)

4.   For civil commitment describe the underlying principle, common criteria, and common categories of commitment procedures. (p. 621–622)

5.   How dangerous are former mental patients? Describe and evaluate traditional research on predicting dangerousness. What practical criteria are used? How have these principles been extended in the case of sex offenders? (p. 622–625)

6.   Summarize the recent trend in voluntary/involuntary hospital admissions. Why are courts protecting rights of individuals admitted to mental hospitals? (p. 625–629)

7.   Summarize three recent trends protecting the rights of individuals who have been committed. How do ethical free will issues underlie these trends? How do Paul and Lentz propose to deal with these seemingly contradictory rights? (p. 629–635)

8.   What factors led to deinstitutionalization policies? What were the unintended results? What future do Gralnick and others fear? (p. 635–637)

Ethical Dilemmas in Therapy and Research (p. 637–647)

9.   Give three examples outside psychology that point to the need for ethical restraints in research. In current research, what process protects participants, and what two recent developments threaten that protection? (p. 637–639)

10.   Summarize five ethical dilemmas (starting with "Informed Consent"). Explain why each is a dilemma (i.e. why the ethically correct decision may be unclear). (p. 639–646) Distinguish, especially, between confidentiality and privileged communication (on p. 641).

11.   Summarize the ethical and legal issues involved in reports of recovered memories. Summarize the textbook's concluding comments. (p. 646–647)

Self-test, Chapter 18

(* Items not covered in Study Questions.)

Multiple-choice

1. The insanity defense in the courtroom originated
   a. from the ideas of Hippocrates.
   b. in the 14th century.
   c. around the time of the Civil War.
   d. in the early 20th century.

2. What is the rationale of laws that provide for legal verdicts of "guilty but mentally ill"?
   a. To prevent the truly insane from being treated as criminals.
   b. To provide treatment options for convicted criminals while still holding them responsible for their actions.
   c. To deal with mentally ill vagrants.
   d. To permit consideration of whether the accused could appreciate the wrongfulness of his or her actions.

3. The issue of competency to stand trial is based on the basic legal principle
   a. that trials should not occur without the accused being present.
   b. that mentally ill persons may not be responsible for their crimes.
   c. of innocent until proven guilty.
   d. of free will and the knowledge of right and wrong.

4. Most states hold that a person can be involuntarily committed to a mental hospital
   a. if found to be mentally ill.
   b. if found to be both mentally ill and dangerous.
   c. only if he or she has committed a crime.
   d. only if he or she has committed a violent crime.

5. The prediction of dangerousness is probably best
   a. when the person is experiencing hallucinations.
   b. when predictions are made during emergency situations.
   c. following extended hospitalizations.
   d. after a period of relative calm.

*6. The Tarasoff case led to the ruling that a therapist who learns that a client is threatening to harm someone
   a. must take steps to have the person committed.
   b. must physically detain the client.
   c. must warn the intended victim of the client.
   d. must break confidentiality and notify police or other authorities that the person is dangerous.

7. Which of the following is *true* regarding the right to refuse treatment?
   a. It does not apply if a person is judged to be at risk for becoming dangerous to others.
   b. It does not apply if a person is a danger to themselves.
   c. It applies only to those in the least restrictive environment.
   d. It applies to criminal commitment but not civil commitment.

8. Deinstitutionalization has been described as an improper label because
    a. most patients end up in treatment in outpatient clinics, thus visiting other institutions.
    b. most deinstitutionalized patients remain mentally ill.
    c. patients typically end up in other long-term care institutions.
    d. few patients are actually discharged from the hospital.

9. When subjects in research studies are told about the potential risks and are free to decline participation, it is called
    a. informed consent.
    b. freedom of choice.
    c. parens patriae.
    d. mens rea.

10. A major reason for some homosexuals to seek out therapy to change sexual orientation stems from
    a. verbal abuse and physical threats from family and members of the community.
    b. genuine desire to change orientation.
    c. confusion over social roles.
    d. an inability to legally marry in many states.

Short Answer

1. Summarize the case of *Jones v. United States*.

2. What issues underlie synthetic sanity?

3. Suppose your friend becomes very upset but refuses to seek help. He/she is considering suicide. What should you do?

4. How dangerous are former mental patients?

5. Why are courts protecting the rights of individuals threatened with involuntary commitment?

6. What do Gralnick and others fear will happen to deinstitutionalized mental patients?

7. What procedures (supposedly) protects the rights of research participants?

8.   Give several reasons (the text lists four) why therapists may reveal things clients tell them even when state law provides privileged communication for therapy relationships.

9.   Describe the ethical issue of "who is the client".

10. What is the ethical issue in reports of recovered memories of child abuse?

Answers to Self-test, Chapter 18

Multiple-choice

1. b (p. 608)   2. b (p. 613)   3. a (p. 617)   4. b (p. 622)
5. b (p. 623–624)   6. c (p. 626)   7. b (p. 632)   8. c (p. 635–636)
9. a (p. 639–640)   10. a (p. 644)

Short Answer

1. Jones was arrested for a misdemeanor but was found insane. As a result he was hospitalized for longer than he could have been imprisoned if found guilty. Supreme Court ruled it did not matter as he was being treated, not punished. (p. 614–616)

2. Drugs could be used to make a person synthetically sane to stand trial. But the drugs might not work, produce dangerous side effects, give the jury a false impression, etc. (p. 618)

3. Call the police who will pick up your friend and take him/her to a mental hospital to be evaluated for informal civil commitment. (It's likely your friend will understand why you did this once they recover. If they do not — at least they're still alive.) (p. 622)

4. Despite stereotypes, research indicates they are, generally, no more dangerous than people in general. Exception is substance abusers, who are more likely to be dangerous (whether ex-patients or not). (p. 622–623)

5. Courts are enforcing the same due process rights that are granted to individuals threatened with loss of freedom for other reasons (such as those accused of crimes). (p. 625–628)

6. They will be seen as social embarrassments and legal problems. They will be arrested to get them off the streets, given drugs and treated impersonally which is not really helpful or effective. (p. 636–637)

7. Participants have the right to understand any risks of participating in research, to freely consent (or refuse) to participate, and to withdraw at any time. (p. 639–640)

8. (a) Client files suit against therapist, (b) client is being abused, (c) client started therapy to evade law, (d) client is dangerous to self or others. (p. 641)

9. Refers to situations where the therapist has responsibility to several individuals or entities whose interests may differ. Therapist may not be able to serve both interests. (p. 641)

10. Dangers both in encouraging and discouraging clients to recover memories. Encouragement could lead to false diagnosis. Discouragement could mean the memory remains repressed but hampers the client's current life. (p. 646)